CRITICAL

ANTHOLOGY

FOR

OCR AS ENGLISH

LITERATURE

OCR
RECOGNISING ACHIEVEMENT

OXFORD
UNIVERSITY PRESS

Official Publisher Partnership

Oxford University Press is a department of the University of Oxford. It furthers the University's objective
of excellence in research, scholarship, and education by publishing worldwide in

Oxford   New York

Auckland   Cape Town   Dar es Salaam   Hong Kong   Karachi
Kuala Lumpur   Madrid   Melbourne   Mexico City   Nairobi
New Delhi   Shanghai   Taipei   Toronto

With offices in

Argentina   Austria   Brazil   Chile   Czech Republic   France   Greece   Gautamala   Hungary
Italy   Japan   South Korea   Poland   Portugal   Singapore   Switzerland   Thailand   Turkey   Ukraine   Vietnam

Oxford is a registered trade mark of Oxford University Press
in the UK and in certain other countries

British Library Cataloguing in Publication Data

Data available

ISBN: 978-0-19-838696-4

10 9 8 7 6

Printed by Ashford Colour Press Ltd., Gosport.

Paper used in the production of this book is a natural, recyclable product made from wood grown
in sustainable forests. The manufacturing process conforms to the environmental regulations
of the country of origin.

Acknowledgements

We gratefully acknowledge permission to use extracts from the following works in this book.

Robert Eaglestone: *Doing English* (2e, Routledge, 2002), copyright © Robert Eaglestone 2000, reprinted by
permission of Taylor & Francis Books UK.

David Lodge: *The Art of Fiction* (Penguin, 1992), copyright © David Lodge 1992, reprinted by permission of Curtis
Brown Group Ltd, London, on behalf of David Lodge.

Martin Montgomery, Alan Durant, Nigel Fabb, Tom Furniss and **Sara Mills**: *Ways of Reading* (3e, Routledge,
2007), copyright © Martin Montgomery, Alan Durant, Nigel Fabb, Tom Furniss and Sara Mills 1992, 2007, reprinted
by permission of Taylor & Francis Books UK.

Malcolm Peet and David Robinson: *Leading Questions* (Nelson Thornes, 2004), copyright © Malcolm Peet and
David Robinson 1992, reprinted by permission of the publishers.

And for the following works used within the above:

Paul Auster: extracts from *The New York Trilogy* (Faber, 1988), copyright © Paul Auster 1988, reprinted by
permission of the publishers.

Wendy Cope: 'Reading Scheme' from *Making Cocoa for Kingsley Amis* (Faber, 1986), copyright © Wendy Cope 1986,
reprinted by permission of the publishers.

Ernest Hemingway: 'A Very Short Story' from *The First Forty Nine Stories by Ernest Hemingway* (Jonathan Cape, 1944),
reprinted by permission of The Random House Group Ltd.

George V Higgins: extract from *Kennedy for the Defense* (Martin Secker & Warburg, 1980), copyright © George V
Higgins 1980, reprinted by permission of The Albert LaFarge Literary Agency.

Ogden Nash: 'The Octopus' from *Candy is Dandy: The Best of Ogden Nash* (Andre Deutsch, 1994), reprinted by
permission of the publishers, the Carlton Publishing Group.

Henry Wade: extract from 'The Three Keys', copyright © Henry Wade 1981, from *The Fifth Bedside Book of Great
Detective Stories* edited by Herbert van Thal (Arthur Barker Ltd, 1981), reprinted by permission of A M Heath & Co
Ltd, Author's Agents.

H G Wells: extract from *War of the Worlds* (1924), reprinted by permission of A P Watt Ltd on behalf of The Literary
Executors of the Estate of H G Wells.

We have made every effort to trace and contact copyright holders before publication. If notified, the publisher will
rectify any errors or omissions at the earliest opportunity.

Contents

OCR Specification Excerpt

The OCR GCE specification for English Literature is the document on which assessment is based; it specifies the content and skills to be covered in delivering a course of study. At all times, therefore, these excerpts should be read in conjunction with the specification. If clarification on a particular point is needed then reference should be in the first instance to the specification.

Unit Content

AS Unit F661: *Poetry and Prose 1800–1945* (Closed text)

- Section A: Poetry 1800–1945
- *Section B: Prose 1800–1945*

Section B: Prose 1800–1945

The focus of this section is the study of a prose set text from the period 1800–1945. There is a choice of **two** questions on each set text and candidates answer **one** question on the text they have studied.

Candidates should be able to:

- respond to a proposition offered in the question demonstrating understanding of the text in relation to the view presented;
- explore how themes and issues are presented, taking into account the effects of language, form and structure.

In this section, study of the chosen text must be complemented by study of a literary-critical text, such as the ones recommended. Study of the 'complementary text' will not be tested in a separate task, but candidates will be expected to demonstrate understanding of basic literary-critical concepts and approaches as presented in these texts. Propositions for tasks in this section may be drawn (or adapted) from these texts.

Complementary literary critical texts supporting Section B: Prose
The following texts are recommended to support reading and understanding of the set texts for Section B: Prose. Teachers and candidates may find it useful to refer to selected sections or chapters rather than to cover the whole text.

Montgomery/Durant/Fabb/Furniss/Mills – *Ways of Reading*, Routledge (978 0415346344)
Malcolm Peet and David Robinson – *Leading Questions*, Nelson (0 174 323379)
Robert Eaglestone – *Doing English*, Routledge (0 415 28423 6)
David Lodge – *The Art of Fiction*, Penguin (0 140 17492 3)

AS GCE Scheme of Assessment

AS Unit F661: Poetry and Prose 1800–1945

60% of the total AS GCE marks
2 h written paper 60 marks

Section B: Prose

Candidates are required to answer **one** question from a choice of two to demonstrate knowledge and understanding of a literary text in relation to an interpretation presented and the significance of social and cultural factors. Candidates are assessed on:

AO1: articulate creative, informed and relevant responses to literary texts, using appropriate terminology and concepts, and coherent, accurate written expression;

AO2: demonstrate detailed critical understanding in analysing the ways in which structure, form and language shape meanings in literary texts;

AO3: explore connections and comparisons between different literary texts, informed by interpretations of other readers;

AO4: demonstrate understanding of the significance and influence of the contexts in which literary texts are written and received.

Assessment Criteria for AS Unit F661: *Poetry and Prose 1800–1945*

Band	AO	Criteria
Band 6 **26–30 marks**	AO 1	• excellent and consistently detailed understanding of texts and question; • consistently fluent, precise writing in appropriate register; • critical terminology used accurately and consistently; • well-structured, coherent and detailed argument consistently developed.
	AO 2	• well-developed and consistently detailed discussion of effects of language, form and structure; • excellent and consistently effective use of analytical methods; • consistently effective use of quotations and references to text, critically addressed, blended into discussion.
	AO 3	• well-developed and consistently effective discussion of relationships between texts; • judgement consistently informed by exploration of different readings of text.
	AO 4	• consistently developed and consistently detailed understanding of the significance and influence of contexts in which literary texts are written and understood, as appropriate to the question.
Band 5 **21–25 marks**	AO 1	• good and secure understanding of texts and question; • good level of coherence and accuracy in writing, in appropriate register; • critical terminology used accurately; • well-structured argument with clear line of development.
	AO 2	• developed and good level of detail in discussion of effects of language, form and structure; • good use of analytical methods; • good use of quotations and references to text, generally critically addressed.
	AO 3	• good, clear discussion of relationships between texts; • good level of recognition and exploration of different readings of texts.
	AO 4	• good, clear evaluation of the significance and influence of contexts in which literary texts are written and understood, as appropriate to the question.
Band 4 **16–20 marks**	AO 1	• competent understanding of texts and question; • clear writing in generally appropriate register; • critical terminology used appropriately; • straightforward arguments generally competently structured.
	AO 2	• generally developed discussion of effects of language, form and structure; • competent use of analytical methods; • competent use of illustrative quotations and references to support discussion.
	AO 3	• competent discussion of relationships between texts; • answer informed by some reference to different readings of texts.
	AO 4	• competent understanding of the significance and influence of contexts in which literary texts are written and understood, as appropriate to the question.
Band 3 **11–15 marks**	AO 1	• some understanding of texts and main elements of question; • some clear writing, some inconsistencies in register; • some appropriate use of critical terminology; • some structured argument evident, lacking development and/or full illustration.
	AO 2	• some attempt to develop discussion of effects of language, form and structure; • some attempt at using analytical methods; • some use of quotations/references as illustration.
	AO 3	• some attempt to develop discussion of relationships between texts; • some awareness of different readings of texts.
	AO 4	• some understanding of the significance and influence of contexts in which literary texts are written and understood, as appropriate to the question.

Band 2 **6–10 marks**	AO 1	• limited understanding of texts and partial attempt at question; • inconsistent writing, frequent instances of technical error, limited use of appropriate register; • limited use of critical terminology; • limited attempt to structure discussion; tendency to lose track of argument.
	AO 2	• limited discussion of effects of language, form and structure; • descriptive or narrative comment; limited use of analytical methods; • limited or inconsistent use of quotations, uncritically presented.
	AO 3	• limited discussion of relationships between texts; • limited awareness of different readings of texts.
	AO 4	• limited understanding of the significance and influence of contexts in which literary texts are written and understood, as appropriate to the question.
Band 1 **0–5 marks**	AO 1	• very little or no connection with texts, question disregarded; • persistent serious writing errors inhibit communication of meaning, very little or no use of appropriate register; • persistently inaccurate or no use of critical terminology; • undeveloped, very fragmentary discussion.
	AO 2	• very little or no relevant discussion of effects of language, form and structure; • very infrequent commentary; very little or no use of analytical methods; • very few quotations (e.g. one or two) used (and likely to be incorrect), or no quotations used.
	AO 3	• very little or no relevant discussion of relationships between texts; • very little or no relevant awareness of different readings of texts.
	AO 4	• very little reference to (and likely to be irrelevant) or no understanding of the significance and influence of contexts in which literary texts are written and understood, as appropriate to the question.

THE ART OF FICTION

1

Beginning

Emma Woodhouse, handsome, clever, and rich, with a comfortable home and happy disposition, seemed to unite some of the best blessings of existence; and had lived nearly twenty-one years in the world with very little to distress or vex her.

She was the youngest of the two daughters of a most affectionate, indulgent father, and had, in consequence of her sister's marriage, been mistress of his house from a very early period. Her mother had died too long ago for her to have more than an indistinct remembrance of her caresses, and her place had been supplied by an excellent woman as governess, who had fallen little short of a mother in affection.

Sixteen years had Miss Taylor been in Mr Woodhouse's family, less as a governess than a friend, very fond of both daughters, but particularly of Emma. Between *them* it was more the intimacy of sisters. Even before Miss Taylor had ceased to hold the nominal office of governess, the mildness of her temper had hardly allowed her to impose any restraint; and the shadow of authority being now long passed away, they had been living together as friend and friend very mutually attached, and Emma doing just what she liked; highly esteeming Miss Taylor's judgment, but directed chiefly by her own.

The real evils indeed of Emma's situation were the power of having rather too much her own way, and a disposition to think a little too well of herself; these were the disadvantages which threatened alloy to her many enjoyments. The danger, however, was at present so unperceived, that they did not by any means rank as misfortunes with her.

Sorrow came – a gentle sorrow – but not at all in the shape of any disagreeable consciousness. – Miss Taylor married.

JANE AUSTEN Emma (1816)

This is the saddest story I have ever heard. We had known the Ashburnhams for nine seasons of the town of Nauheim with an extreme intimacy – or, rather, with an acquaintanceship as loose and easy and yet as close as a good glove's with your hand. My wife and I knew Captain and Mrs Ashburnham as well as it was possible to know anybody, and yet, in another sense, we knew nothing at all about them. This is, I believe, a state of things only possible with English people of whom, till today, when I sit down to puzzle out what I know of this sad affair, I knew nothing whatever. Six months ago I had never been to England, and, certainly, I had never sounded the depths of an English heart. I had known the shallows.

FORD MADOX FORD The Good Soldier (1915)

WHEN DOES A NOVEL BEGIN? The question is almost as difficult to answer as the question, when does the human embryo become a person? Certainly the creation of a novel rarely begins with the penning or typing of its first words. Most writers do some preliminary work, if it is only in their heads. Many prepare the ground carefully over weeks or months, making diagrams of the plot, compiling c.v.s for their characters, filling a notebook with ideas, settings, situations, jokes, to be drawn on in the process of composition. Every writer has his or her own way of working. Henry James made notes for *The Spoils of Poynton* almost as long and almost as interesting as the finished novel. Muriel Spark, I understand, broods mentally on the concept of a new novel and does not set pen to paper until she has thought of a satisfactory opening sentence.

For the reader, however, the novel always begins with that opening sentence (which may not, of course, be the first sentence the novelist originally wrote). And then the next sentence, and then the sentence after that . . . When does the beginning of a novel end, is another difficult question to answer. Is it the first paragraph, the first few pages, or the first chapter? However one defines it, the beginning of a novel is a threshold, separating the real world we inhabit from the world the novelist has imagined. It should therefore, as the phrase goes, "draw us in".

This is not an easy task. We are not yet familiar with the author's tone of voice, range of vocabulary, syntactic habits. We read a book slowly and hesitantly, at first. We have a lot of new information to absorb and remember, such as the characters' names, their relationships of affinity and consanguinity, the contextual details of time and place, without which the story cannot be followed. Is all this effort going to be worthwhile? Most readers will give an author the benefit of the doubt for at least a few pages, before deciding to back out over the threshold. With the two specimens shown here, however, our hesitation is likely to be minimal or non-existent. We are "hooked" by the very first sentence in each case.

Jane Austen's opening is classical: lucid, measured, objective, with ironic implication concealed beneath the elegant velvet glove of the style. How subtly the first sentence sets up the heroine for a fall. This is to be the reverse of the Cinderella story, the triumph of an undervalued heroine, that previously attracted Jane Austen's imagination from *Pride and Prejudice* to *Mansfield Park*. Emma is a Princess who must be humbled before she finds true happiness. "Handsome" (rather than conventionally pretty or beautiful – a hint of masculine will-to-power, perhaps, in that androgynous epithet), "clever" (an ambiguous term for intelligence, sometimes applied derogatively, as in "too clever for her own good") and "rich", with all its biblical and proverbial associations of the moral dangers of wealth: these three adjectives, so elegantly combined (a matter of stress and phonology – try rearranging them) encapsulate the deceptiveness of Emma's "seeming" contentment. Having lived "nearly twenty-one years in the world with very little to distress or vex her", she is due for a rude awakening. Nearly twenty-one, the traditional age of majority, Emma must now take responsibility for her own life, and for a woman in early nineteenth-century bourgeois society this meant deciding whether and whom to marry. Emma is unusually free in this respect, since she is already "mistress"of her household, a circumstance likely to breed arrogance, especially as she has been brought up by a governess who supplied a mother's affection but not (by implication) a mother's discipline.

This suggestion is made more emphatically in the third paragraph; but at the same time, interestingly enough, we begin to hear the voice of Emma herself in the discourse, as well as the judicious, objective voice of the narrator. "Between *them* it was more the intimacy of sisters." "They had been living together as friend and friend . . . " In these phrases we seem to hear Emma's own, rather self-satisfied description of her relationship with her governess, one which allowed her to do "just what she liked." The ironic structure of the paragraph's conclusion, "highly esteeming Miss Taylor's judgment, but directed chiefly by her own," symmetrically balances two statements that are logically incompatible, and thus indicates the flaw in Emma's character that is explicitly stated by the narrator in the fourth paragraph. With the marriage of Miss Taylor, the story proper begins: deprived of Miss Taylor's company and mature counsel, Emma takes up a young protégée, Harriet, who encourages her vanity, and on whose behalf she begins to indulge in a matchmaking intrigue, with disastrous results.

Ford Madox Ford's famous opening sentence is a blatant ploy to secure the reader's attention, virtually dragging us over the threshold by the collar. But almost at once a characteristically modern obscurity and indirection, an anxiety about the possibility of discovering any truth, infect the narrative. Who is this person addressing us? He uses English yet is not English himself. He has known the English couple who seem to be the subject of the "saddest story" for at least nine years, yet claims to have "known nothing" about the English until this very moment of narration. "Heard" in the first sentence suggests that he is going to narrate someone else's story, but almost immediately it is implied that the narrator, and perhaps his wife, were themselves part of it. The narrator knows the Ashburnhams intimately – and not at all. These contradictions are rationalized as an effect of Englishness, of the disparity between appearance and reality in English middle-class behaviour; so this beginning strikes a similar thematic note to *Emma*'s, though tragic rather than comic in its premonitory undertones. The word "sad" is repeated towards the end of the paragraph, and another keyword, "heart" (two of the characters have supposed heart-conditions, all of them have disordered emotional lives), is dropped into the penultimate sentence.

I used the metaphor of a glove to describe Jane Austen's style, a style which itself claims authority partly by eschewing metaphor (metaphor being an essentially poetic figure of speech, at the opposite pole to reason and common sense). That same metaphor of a glove actually occurs in the opening paragraph of *The Good Soldier*, though with a different meaning. Here it signifies polite social behaviour, the easy but restrained manners that go with affluence and discriminating taste (a "good" glove is specified), but with a hint of deceptive concealment or "covering up". Some of the enigmas raised in the first paragraph are quickly explained – by, for instance, the information that the narrator is an American living in Europe. But the reliability of his testimony, and the chronic dissembling of the other characters, are to be crucial issues in this, the saddest story.

There are, of course, many other ways of beginning a novel, and it is worth indicating the range of possibilities here. A novel may begin with a set-piece description of a landscape or townscape that is to be the primary setting of the story, the *mise-en-scène* as film criticism terms it: for example, the sombre description of Egdon Heath at the beginning of Thomas Hardy's *The Return of the Native*, or E. M. Forster's account of Chandrapore, in elegant, urbane guide-book prose, at the outset of *A Passage to India*. A novel may begin in the middle of a conversation, like Evelyn Waugh's *A Handful of Dust*, or Ivy Compton-Burnett's idiosyncratic works. It may begin with an arresting self-introduction by the narrator, "Call me

Ishmael" (Herman Melville's *Moby Dick*), or with a rude gesture at the literary tradition of autobiography: ". . . the first thing you'll probably want to know is where I was born, and what my lousy childhood was like, and how my parents were occupied and all before they had me, and all that David Copperfield kind of crap, but I don't feel like going into it" (J. D. Salinger's *The Catcher in the Rye*). A novelist may begin with a philosophical reflection – "The past is a foreign country: they do things differently there" (L. P. Hartley, *The Go-Between*), or pitch a character into extreme jeopardy with the very first sentence: "Hale knew they meant to murder him before he had been in Brighton three hours" (Graham Greene, *Brighton Rock*). Many novels begin with a "frame-story" which explains how the main story was discovered, or describes it being told to a fictional audience. In Conrad's *Heart of Darkness* an anonymous narrator describes Marlow relating his Congo experiences to a circle of friends sitting on the deck of a cruising yawl in the Thames estuary ("And this also," Marlow begins, "has been one of the dark places of the earth"). Henry James's *The Turn of the Screw* consists of a deceased woman's memoir, which is read aloud to guests at a country-house party who have been entertaining themselves with ghost stories, and get, perhaps, more than they bargained for. Kingsley Amis begins his ghost story, *The Green Man,* with a witty pastiche of the *The Good Food Guide*: "No sooner has one got over one's surprise at finding a genuine coaching inn less than 40 miles from London – and 8 from the M1 – than one is marvelling at the quality of the equally English fare . . ." Italo Calvino's *If on a winter's night a traveller* begins, "You are about to begin reading Italo Calvino's new novel, *If on a winter's night a traveller.*" James Joyce's *Finnegans Wake* begins in the middle of a sentence: "riverrun, past Eve and Adam's, from swerve of shore to bend of bay, brings us by a commodius vicus of recirculation back to Howth Castle and Environs." The missing fragment concludes the book: "A way a lone a last a loved a long the" – thus returning us to the beginning again, like the recirculation of water in the environment, from river to sea to cloud to rain to river, and like the unending production of meaning in the reading of fiction.

2

Introducing a Character

A few minutes later, Sally herself arrived.

"Am I terribly late, Fritz darling?"

"Only half of an hour, I suppose," Fritz drawled, beaming with proprietary pleasure. "May I introduce Mr Isherwood – Miss Bowles? Mr Isherwood is commonly known as Chris."

"I'm not," I said. "Fritz is about the only person who's ever called me Chris in my life."

Sally laughed. She was dressed in black silk, with a small cape over her shoulders and a little cap like a page-boy's stuck jauntily on one side of her head:

"Do you mind if I use your telephone, sweet?"

"Sure. Go right ahead." Fritz caught my eye. "Come into the other room, Chris. I want to show you something." He was evidently longing to hear my first impressions of Sally, his new acquisition.

"For heaven's sake, don't leave me alone with this man!" she exclaimed. "Or he'll seduce me down the telephone. He's most terribly passionate."

As she dialled the number, I noticed that her finger-nails were painted emerald green, a colour unfortunately chosen, for it called attention to her hands, which were much stained by cigarette-smoking and as dirty as a little girl's. She was dark enough to be Fritz's sister. Her face was long and thin, powdered dead white. She had very large brown eyes which should have been darker, to match her hair and the pencil she used for her eyebrows.

"Hilloo," she cooed, pursing her brilliant cherry lips as though she were going to kiss the mouthpiece: "Ist dass Du, mein Liebling?" Her

**mouth opened in a fatuously sweet smile. Fritz and I sat watching
her, like a performance at the theatre.**

CHRISTOPHER ISHERWOOD Goodbye to Berlin (1939)

CHARACTER is arguably the most important single component of the
novel. Other narrative forms, such as epic, and other media, such
as film, can tell a story just as well, but nothing can equal the great
tradition of the European novel in the richness, variety and psychological depth of its portrayal of human nature. Yet character
is probably the most difficult aspect of the art of fiction to discuss
in technical terms. This is partly because there are so many different types of character and so many different ways of representing
them: major characters and minor characters, flat characters and
round characters, characters rendered from inside their minds, like
Virginia Woolf's Mrs Dalloway, and characters viewed from outside
by others, like Christopher Isherwood's Sally Bowles.

Originally the subject of one of the lightly fictionalized stories and
sketches that make up *Goodbye to Berlin*, Sally Bowles has enjoyed a
remarkably long life in the public imagination of our time, thanks to
the successful adaption of Isherwood's text first as a stage play and
film (*I Am A Camera*), then as a stage and film musical (*Cabaret*). At
first glance, it's hard to understand why she should have achieved
this almost mythical status. She is not particularly beautiful, not
particularly intelligent, and not particularly gifted as an artiste. She
is vain, feckless, and mercenary in her sexual relationships. But she
retains an endearing air of innocence and vulnerability in spite of it
all, and there is something irresistibly comic about the gap between
her pretensions and the facts of her life. Her story gains enormously
in interest and significance from being set in Weimar Berlin, just before the Nazi takeover. Dreaming vainly of fame and riches in seedy
lodging houses, bouncing from one *louche* protector to another, flat-
tering, exploiting and lying, in the most transparent fashion, she is
an emblem of the self-deception and folly of that doomed society.

The simplest way to introduce a character, common in older fiction, is to give a physical description and biographical summary. The portrait of Dorothea Brooke in the first chapter of George Eliot's *Middlemarch* is a consummate example of this method:

> Miss Brooke had that kind of beauty which seems to be thrown into relief by poor dress. Her hand and wrist were so finely formed that she could wear sleeves not less bare of style than those in which the Blessed Virgin appeared to Italian painters; and her profile as well as her stature and bearing seemed to gain the more dignity from her plain garments, which by the side of provincial fashion gave her the impressiveness of a fine quotation from the Bible – or from one of our elder poets – in a paragraph of today's newspaper. She was usually spoken of as being remarkably clever, but with the addition that her sister Celia had more common sense.

And so on, for several pages. It is magnificent, but it belongs to a more patient and leisurely culture than ours. Modern novelists usually prefer to let the facts about a character emerge gradually, diversified, or actually conveyed, by action and speech. In any case, all description in fiction is highly selective; its basic rhetorical technique is synecdoche, the part standing for the whole. Both George Eliot and Christopher Isherwood evoke the physical appearance of their heroines by focusing on the hands and the face, leaving the reader to imagine the rest. An exhaustive description of Dorothea's or Sally Bowles's physical and psychological attributes would take many pages, perhaps an entire book.

Clothes are always a useful index of character, class, life-style, but especially in the case of an exhibitionist like Sally. Her black silk get-up (worn for a casual afternoon visit) signals desire-to-impress, theatricality (the cape), and sexual provocativeness (the page-boy's hat acquires connotations from the many references to sexual ambivalence and deviation, including transvestism, that run through the book). These traits are immediately reinforced by her speech and behaviour – asking to use the telephone in order to impress the two men with her latest erotic conquest – which then gives the narrator the opportunity for a description of Sally's hands and face.

This is what Henry James meant by the "scenic method", what he aimed to achieve when he exhorted himself to "Dramatize! dramatize!" James was thinking of the stage play, but Isherwood belonged to the first generation of novelists to grow up with the cinema, and its influence shows. When the narrator of *Goodbye to Berlin* says "I am a camera," he is thinking of a movie camera. Whereas Dorothea is posed statically, as if sitting for a verbal portrait, and is actually compared to a figure in a painting, Sally is shown to us *in action.* It is easy to break down this passage into a sequence of cinematic shots: Sally posing in her black silk outfit – a quick exchange of glances between the two men – a close-up of Sally's green fingernails as she dials the number – another close-up of her ill-coordinated, clown-like makeup and affected expression as she greets her lover – and a two-shot of the male spectators, riveted by the sheer ham of the performance.

No doubt this partly explains the ease with which Sally Bowles's story has transferred to the screen. But there are nuances in the passage which are purely literary. Those green fingernails on grubby hands are what I first think of when her name is mentioned. You could show the green nail-polish in a film, but not the narrator's ironic comment, "a colour unfortunately chosen". "Unfortunately chosen" is the story of Sally Bowles's life. And you could show the cigarette stains and the dirt, but only a narrator could observe, "dirty as a little girl's". The childlike quality beneath the surface sophistication is precisely what makes Sally Bowles a memorable character.

3

Irony

Her face, viewed so close that he could see the almost imperceptible down on those fruit-like cheeks, was astonishingly beautiful; the dark eyes were exquisitely misted; and he could feel the secret loyalty of her soul ascending to him. She was very slightly taller than her lover; but somehow she hung from him, her body curved backwards, and her bosom pressed against his, so that instead of looking up at her gaze he looked down at it. He preferred that; perfectly proportioned though he was, his stature was a delicate point with him. His spirits rose by the uplift of his senses. His fears slipped away; he began to be very satisfied with himself. He was the inheritor of twelve thousand pounds, and he had won this unique creature. She was his capture; he held her close, permittedly scanning the minutiae of her skin, permittedly crushing her flimsy silks. Something in him had forced her to lay her modesty on the altar of his desire. And the sun brightly shone. So he kissed her yet more ardently, and with the slightest touch of a victor's condescension; and her burning response more than restored the self-confidence which he had been losing.

"I've got no one but you now," she murmured in a melting voice.

She fancied in her ignorance that the expression of this sentiment would please him. She was not aware that a man is usually rather chilled by it, because it proves to him that the other is thinking about his responsibilities and not about his privileges. Certainly it calmed Gerald, though without imparting to him her sense of his responsibilites. He smiled vaguely. To Sophia his smile was a miracle continually renewed; it mingled dashing gaiety with a hint of wistful appeal

in a manner that never failed to bewitch her. A less innocent girl
than Sophia might have divined from that adorable half-feminine
smile that she could do anything with Gerald except rely on him. But
Sophia had to learn.

ARNOLD BENNETT The Old Wives' Tale (1908)

IN RHETORIC, irony consists of saying the opposite of what you mean,
or inviting an interpretation different from the surface meaning of
your words. Unlike other figures of speech – metaphor, simile, me-
tonymy, synecdoche, etc. – irony is not distinguished from literal
statement by any peculiarity of verbal form. An ironic statement is
recognized as such in the act of interpretation. When, for example,
the authorial narrator of *Pride and Prejudice says*, "It is a truth universally acknowledged, that a single man in possession of a fortune,
must be in want of a wife," the reader, alerted by the false logic of
the proposition about single men with fortunes, interprets the "uni-
versal" generalization as an ironic comment on a particular social
group obsessed with matchmaking. The same rule applies to action
in narrative. When the reader is made aware of a disparity between
the facts of a situation and the characters' understanding of it, an
effect called "dramatic irony" is generated. It has been said that all
novels are essentially about the passage from innocence to experience, about discovering the reality that underlies appearances. It
is not surprising, therefore, that stylistic and dramatic irony are
all-pervasive in this form of literature. Most of the passages I discuss
could be analysed under the heading of Irony.

Arnold Bennett employs two different methods in this passage
from *The Old Wives' Tale* to put his characters' behaviour in an
ironic perspective. Sophia, the beautiful, passionate but inexperi-
enced daughter of a draper in the Potteries, is sufficiently dazzled by
Gerald Scales, a handsome commercial traveller who has inherited
a small fortune, to elope with him. The embrace described here is
their first in the privacy of their London lodgings. What should be

a moment of erotic rapture and emotional unity is revealed as the physical conjunction of two people whose thoughts are running on quite different tracks.

Gerald in fact intends to seduce Sophia, though in the event he lacks the self-assurance to carry out his plan. Even in this embrace he is at first nervous and tentative, "perceiving that her ardour was exceeding his." But as the intimate contact continues, he becomes more confident and masterful. There is probably a sexual pun hidden in "His spirits rose by the uplift of his senses," for Bennett frequently hinted in this fashion at things he dared not describe explicitly. Gerald's sexual arousal has nothing to do with love, however, or even lust. It is a function of his vanity and self-esteem. "Something in him had forced her to lay her modesty on the altar of his desire." Like "the secret loyalty of her soul ascending to him" earlier, this florid metaphor mocks the complacent thought it expresses. The use of the word "altar" carries an extra ironic charge since at this point Gerald has no intention of leading Sophia to the altar of marriage.

Up to this point, Bennett keeps to Gerald's point of view, and uses the kind of language appropriate to that perspective, thus *implying* an ironic assessment of Gerald's character. The description of his timidity, vanity and complacency – so very different from what he *ought* to be feeling in this situation – and the slightly absurd, inflated rhetoric in which he represents his emotions to himself, are enough to condemn him in the reader's eyes. In the second paragraph, however, Bennett uses the convention of the omniscient intrusive author to switch to Sophia's point of view, and to comment explicitly on her misconceptions, adding to the layers of irony in the scene.

Sophia's thoughts are more creditable than Gerald's, but her words, "I've got no one but you now," are partly calculated to endear him to her. This merely reveals her naivety, however. As the "burning" Sophia utters this sentiment in a "melting" voice, Gerald is "chilled" by the reminder of his responsibilities. He responds with a non-committal smile, which the infatuated Sophia finds charming, but which, the narrator assures us, was an index of his unreliability and a portent of disillusionment to come. The authorial voice, dry, precise, urbane, overrides the "inner voice" of Sophia to expose the fallibility of her judgment.

The reader, privileged with knowledge denied to the participants in the scene, looks over the author's shoulder with pity for Sophia and contempt for Gerald. One of Bennett's *Notebook* entries reads, rather surprisingly, "Essential characteristic of the really great novelist: a Christ-like, all-embracing compassion"; his treatment of Gerald fell short of that high standard. This type of irony leaves us with little work of inference or interpretation to do; on the contrary, we are the passive recipients of the author's worldly wisdom. If the effect does not seem as heavy-handed as it easily might, that is because the acuteness of Bennett's psychological observation earns our respect, and because he allows characters like Sophia to "learn" from their mistakes, and survive them.

4

Ending

The anxiety, which in this state of their attachment must be the portion of Henry and Catherine, and of all who loved either, as to its final event, can hardly extend, I fear, to the bosom of my readers, who will see in the tell-tale compression of the pages before them, that we are all hastening together to perfect felicity.

JANE AUSTEN Northanger Abbey (1818)

Ralph looked at him dumbly. For a moment he had a fleeting picture of the strange glamour that had once invested the beaches. But the island was scorched up like dead wood – Simon was dead – and Jack had . . . The tears began to flow and sobs shook him. He gave himself up to them now for the first time on the island; great, shuddering spasms of grief that seemed to wrench his whole body. His voice rose under the black smoke before the burning wreckage of the island; and infected by that emotion, the other little boys began to shake and sob too. And in the middle of them, with filthy body, matted hair, and unwiped nose, Ralph wept for the end of innocence, the darkness of man's heart, and the fall through the air of the true, wise friend called Piggy.

The officer, surrounded by these noises, was moved and a little embarrassed. He turned away to give them time to pull themselves together; and waited, allowing his eyes to rest on the trim cruiser in the distance.

WILLIAM GOLDING Lord of the Flies (1954)

"CONCLUSIONS are the weak points of most authors," George Eliot remarked, "but some of the fault lies in the very nature of a conclusion, which is at best a negation." To Victorian novelists endings were apt to be particularly troublesome, because they were always under pressure from readers and publishers to provide a happy one. The last chapter was known in the trade as the "wind-up", which Henry James sarcastically described as "a distribution at the last of prizes, pensions, husbands, wives, babies, millions, appended paragraphs and cheerful remarks." James himself pioneered the "open" ending characteristic of modern fiction, often stopping the novel in the middle of a conversation, leaving a phrase hanging resonantly, but ambiguously, in the air: "'Then there we are,' said Strether." (*The Ambassadors*)

As Jane Austen pointed out in a metafictional aside in *Northanger Abbey*, a novelist cannot conceal the timing of the end of the story (as a dramatist or film-maker can, for instance) because of the telltale compression of the pages. When John Fowles provides a mock-Victorian wind-up to *The French Lieutenant's Woman* (in which Charles settles down happily with Ernestina) we are not deceived, for a quarter of the book remains to be read. Going on with the story of Charles's quest for Sarah, Fowles offers us two more alternative endings – one that ends happily for the hero, and the other unhappily. He invites us to choose between them, but tacitly encourages us to see the second as more authentic, not just because it is sadder, but because it is more open, with the sense of life going on into an uncertain future.

Perhaps we should distinguish between the end of a novel's story – the resolution or deliberate non-resolution of the narrative questions it has raised in the minds of its readers – and the last page or two of the text, which often act as a kind of epilogue or postscript, a gentle deceleration of the discourse as it draws to a halt. But this scarcely applies to the novels of Sir William Golding, whose last pages have a way of throwing everything that has gone before into a new and surprising light. *Pincher Martin* (1956), for instance, seems to be the story of a torpedoed sailor's desperate and finally

unsuccessful struggle to survive on a bare rock in the middle of the
Atlantic, but the final chapter reveals that he died with his boots
on – so the whole narrative must be reinterpreted as some kind of
drowning vision or purgatorial experience after death. The ending
of *The Paper Men* (1984) reserves its final punch till the narrator's
very last word, which is interrupted by a bullet: "How the devil did
Rick L. Tucker manage to get hold of a gu "

That kind of last-minute twist is generally more typical of the
short story than of the novel. Indeed one might say that the short
story is essentially "end-oriented", inasmuch as one begins a short
story in the expectation of soon reaching its conclusion, whereas
one embarks upon a novel with no very precise idea of when one
will finish it. We tend to read a short story in a single sitting, drawn
along by the magnetic power of its anticipated conclusion; whereas
we pick up and put down a novel at irregular intervals, and may be
positively sorry to come to the end of it. Novelists of old used to exploit this sentimental bond formed between the reader and the novel
during the reading experience. Fielding, for instance begins the last
Book of *Tom Jones* with "A Farewell to the Reader":

> We are now, reader, arrived at the last stage of our long journey. As we
> have therefore, travelled together through so many pages, let us be-
> have to one another like fellow-travellers, in a stage coach, who have
> passed several days in the company of each other; and who, notwith-
> standing any bickerings or little animosities which may have occurred
> on the road, generally make up at last, and mount, for the last time,
> into their vehicle with cheerfulness and good humour; since after this
> one stage it may possibly happen to us, as it commonly happens to
> them, never to meet more.

The conclusion of *The Lord of the Flies* could easily have been a
comfortable and reassuring one, because it introduces an adult
perspective in the last few pages of what, up to that point, has been
a "boys' story", a *Coral Island*-style adventure, that goes horribly
wrong. A party of British schoolboys, who crash-land on a tropical
island in unspecified circumstances (though there are hints of a

war), rapidly revert to savagery and superstition. Freed from the restraints of civilized, adult society, and subject to hunger, loneliness and fear, the behaviour of the playground degenerates into tribal violence. Two boys die, and the hero, Ralph, is fleeing for his life from a pack of bloodthirsty pursuers wielding wooden spears, and a deliberately started forest fire, when he runs full-tilt into a naval officer who has just landed on the beach, his ship alerted by the smoke. "Fun and games," the officer comments, regarding the boys with their makeshift weapons and warpaint.

For the reader, the apparition of the officer is almost as startling, and almost as great a relief, as it is for Ralph. We have been so absorbed in the story, and so involved in Ralph's plight, that we have forgotten that he and his cruel enemies are prepubescent boys. Suddenly, through the officer's eyes, we see them for what they really are, a bunch of dirty and unkempt children. But Golding does not allow this effect to undermine the essential truth of what has gone before, or make the restoration of "normality" into a comforting happy ending. The naval officer will never comprehend the experience that Ralph (and vicariously the reader) has undergone, eloquently recapitulated in the penultimate paragraph: "the end of innocence, the darkness of man's heart, and the fall through the air of the true, wise friend called Piggy." He will never understand why Ralph's sobbing spreads infectiously through the other boys. "He turned away, to give them time to pull themselves together; and waited, allowing his eyes to rest on the trim cruiser in the distance." The last sentence of any story acquires a certain resonance merely by virtue of being the last, but this one is particularly rich in irony. The adult's gaze at the "trim cruiser" implies complacency, evasion of the truth, and complicity in an institutionalized form of violence – modern warfare – that is equivalent to, as well as different from, the primitive violence of the castaway boys.

Readers acquainted with my *Changing Places* may recall that the passage from *Northanger Abbey* at the head of this chapter is cited by

Philip Swallow and quoted by Morris Zapp on the last page of that novel. Philip invokes it to illustrate an important difference between an audience's experience of the end of a film, and a reader's experience of the end of a novel:

> "That's something the novelist can't help giving away, isn't it, that his novel is shortly coming to an end? . . . he can't disguise the tell-tale compression of the pages . . . As you're reading, you're aware that there's only a page or two left in the book, and you get ready to close it. But with a film there's no way of telling, especially nowadays, when films are much more loosely structured, much more ambivalent, than they used to be. There's no way of telling which frame is going to be the last. The film is going along, just as life goes along, people are be-having, doing things, drinking, talking, and we're watching them, and at any point the director chooses, without warning, without any-thing being resolved, or explained, or wound up, it can just . . . end."

At this point in the book, Philip is represented as a character in a filmscript, and immediately after his speech the novel ends, thus:

PHILIP shrugs. The camera stops, freezing him in mid-gesture.

THE END

I ended the novel in this fashion for several, interrelated reasons. In one aspect, it is a sexual comedy of "long-range wifeswapping": the story concerns the fortunes of two academics, one British and one American, who, exchanging jobs in 1969, have affairs with each other's wives. But the two principal characters exchange much else in the course of the story – values, attitudes, language – and almost every incident in one location has its analogue or mirror-image in the other. Developing this highly symmetrical and perhaps predict-able plot, I felt the need to provide some variety and surprise for the reader on another level of the text, and accordingly wrote each chapter in a different style or format. The first shift is comparatively inconspicuous – from present-tense narration in Chapter One to past-tense narration in Chapter Two. But the third chapter is in epistolary form, and the fourth consists of extracts from newspapers and other documents the characters are supposed to be reading. The fifth chapter is conventional in style, but deviates from the cross-cutting pattern of the previous chapters, presenting the interconnected experiences of the two main characters in consecutive chunks.

As the novel progressed I became increasingly conscious of the problem of how to end it in a way which would be satisfying on both the formal and the narrative levels. As regards the former, it was obvious that the final chapter must exhibit the most striking and surprising shift in narrative form, or risk being an aesthetic anticlimax. As regards the narrative level, I found myself unwilling to resolve the wife-swapping plot, partly because that would mean also resolving the cultural plot. A decision by Philip to stick with Desirée Zapp, for instance, would also entail a decision by him to stay in America or a willingness on her part to settle in England, and so on. I did not want to have to decide, as implied author, in favour of this partnership or that, this culture or that. But how could I "get away with" an ending of radical indeterminacy for a plot that had up till then been as regular and symmetrical in structure as a quadrille?

The idea of writing the last chapter (which is called "Ending") in the form of a filmscript seemed to solve all these problems at a stroke. First of all, such a format satisfied the need for a climactic deviation from "normal" fictional discourse. Secondly it freed me, as implied author, from the obligation to pass judgment on, or to arbitrate between, the claims of the four main characters, since there is no textual trace of the author's voice in a filmscript, consisting as it does of dialogue and impersonal, objective descriptions of the characters' outward behaviour. Philip, Desirée, Morris and Hilary meet in New York, halfway between the West Coast of America and the West Midlands of England, to discuss their marital problems, and in the course of a few days they discuss every possible resolution of the story – each couple to divorce and cross-marry, each couple to reunite, each couple to separate but not remarry, etc. etc. – but without reaching any conclusion. By having Philip draw attention to the fact that films are more amenable to unresolved endings than novels, while being represented as a character in a film inside a novel, I thought I had found a way to justify, by a kind of metafictional joke, my own refusal to resolve the story of *Changing Places*. In fact, so strong – atavistically strong – is the human desire for certainty, resolution and closure, that not all readers were satisfied by this ending, and some have complained to me that they felt cheated by it. But it satisfied *me* (and had the incidental bonus that when I decided to make further use of the principal characters in a subsequent novel, *Small World*, I had a free hand in developing their life-histories).

The point of this anecdote is, however, not to defend the ending of *Changing Places*, but to demonstrate that deciding how to handle it involved many other aspects of the novel. Decisions about particular aspects or components of a novel are never taken in isolation, but affect, and are affected by, all its other aspects and components. A novel is a Gestalt, a German word for which there is no exact English equivalent, but which I define elsewhere as "a perceptual pattern or structure possessing qualities as a whole that cannot be described merely as a sum of its parts."

WAYS OF READING

Irony

1.1 Verbal irony

Verbal irony is a use of language where we do not literally mean what we say; instead we imply an attitude of disbelief towards the content of our utterance or writing. As an example of verbal irony, consider this first sentence of Jane Austen's novel *Pride and Prejudice.*

> It is a truth universally acknowledged, that a single man in possession of a good fortune, must be in want of a wife.

To understand how verbal irony works, we need to consider the construction of the meanings that we communicate when we speak or write. A communicated meaning can be analysed into two component parts: (1) a proposition and (2) an attitude towards that proposition. A proposition is a statement about the real world or about some fictional world. The sentences we produce typically encode propositions by containing specific words in a specific order; to be able to speak and understand sentences of a language is to be able to encode and decode a proposition into and from the sentences of that language. However, both our thoughts and hence the meanings we communicate consist of something more than just basic propositions; attached to each proposition is an attitude, usually known as a propositional attitude, which expresses the speaker's or writer's relation to that proposition. The most common attitude is belief, but there are other attitudes as well – differing in strength (e.g. basic belief as opposed to strong commitment) as well as in polarity (e.g. belief as opposed to disbelief). If I have an attitude of belief towards a proposition, then that proposition is true for me.

This is relevant for irony, because in irony a speaker or writer produces a proposition that is *not* true for him or her. In normal (non-ironic) communication, I communicate two things: a proposition and my attitude towards that proposition, which is that I believe the proposition to be true. In verbal irony, I communicate a proposition and a different kind of attitude: that I do not believe the proposition to be true. There is no difference in the proposition itself; the difference is in the attitude that I communicate. Verbal irony is successful when the writer or speaker provides sufficient evidence to indicate that his or her attitude is one of disbelief rather than the expected attitude of belief. In the quoted sentence from Austen, the author actually communicates two propositions, one inside the other, and makes it clear that she believes neither of them. One proposition is 'a single man in possession of a good fortune, must be in want of a wife', and this proposition is contained inside 'It is a truth universally acknowledged, that a single man in possession of a good fortune, must be in want of a wife.' The larger proposition, by asserting so strongly the truth of the contained proposition, only serves to indicate the writer's own disagreement with both of them.

For irony to function as intended, the writer or speaker must be sure that the reader or hearer will be able to recognize that an attitude of disbelief is being communicated; since this is not the normal state of affairs, there must be something odd about the text in order to give clues that the author disbelieves what he or she is saying. Here the oddness of the text is both in the exaggerated claims to certainty made for the proposition and the fact that the proposition itself is not at all clearly true; for it to be universally acknowledged, we too would have already accepted it as true but we do not.

In irony we should generally interpret the speaker/writer to be saying not only that he or she does not believe the proposition but that someone else might believe it to be true. Thus the ironist communicates, both his or her own attitude (of disbelief) along with implying a different attitude (of belief) attributed to someone else – whether that someone else is identifiable or not. In the case of this proposition, we can straightforwardly assign this thought to one or more of the characters in the novel (and hence partly understand their actions through this belief). Irony often involves the implication that the speaker or writer shares with us an amused attitude towards the misguided characters who believe the proposition.

We now consider another example of verbal irony from George Eliot's novel *Middlemarch* (1871) (discussed in MacCabe (1981)):

> Some who follow the narrative of his experience may wonder at the midnight darkness of Mr Dagley; but nothing was easier in those times than for an hereditary farmer of his grade to be ignorant, in spite somehow of having a rector in the twin parish who was a gentleman to the backbone, a curate nearer at hand who preached more learnedly than the rector, a landlord who had gone into everything, especially fine art and social improvement, and all the lights of Middlemarch only three miles off.

A proposition we can derive from this sentence is 'Given the educated social environment in which he lives, it is surprising that Mr Dagley (the farmer) has remained so ignorant'. We know this to be verbal irony because we know that this proposition is both disbelieved by the writer and attributed to other (misguided, unnamed) people, towards whom the writer has an amused attitude. How do we know that this is irony: that is, that the writer does not hold an attitude of belief towards the proposition? The irony is signalled largely by the exaggerations in the passage: by emphasizing the proposition excessively, the writer warns us that she is not committed to it. There are basically two kinds of exaggeration here: first, expressions of extremity as in 'midnight darkness', 'nothing was easier', 'preached more learnedly than the rector', 'gone into everything', 'all the lights of Middlemarch'; and, second, a repetitive list, stacking up to produce a long sentence. In addition, we probably also bring our knowledge of the world, and perhaps of the novel as it has previously developed, to contradict the proposition derived.

There are different varieties of verbal irony, though all work in basically the same way, whereby an attitude of disbelief is implicitly communicated. Sarcasm is a kind of verbal irony in which, typically, an exaggerated tone of voice communicates the attitude of disbelief. Note however that, while the tone implies disbelief, this is nevertheless implicit: the speaker does not actually *say* that they do not believe what they are saying. In irony the attitude of disbelief is always implicitly communicated rather than explicitly communicated. The first sentence of *Pride and Prejudice* would not be ironic if it was written as 'Some of the characters in this book incorrectly believe that it is a truth universally acknowledged, that a single man in possession of a good fortune, must be in want of a wife.' Irony thus involves some tension between what is said and what is meant.

(A final comment: note that 'verbal' means 'using language' and does not mean the same as 'oral', which means 'using spoken language'; hence verbal irony exists in both speech and writing.)

1.2 Situational irony

Situational irony involves a conflict between what two different people (or two groups of people) know. The participant in events understands them in a way that is not correct, while the viewer or audience to the events understands them differently but correctly, such that their understanding conflicts with the participant's understanding. The viewer or audience is able to do this because they have an advantage over the participant, usually by virtue of being outside the situation of the participant. The participant is 'subject to situational irony', where 'situational irony' can be understood as a way of an audience describing events relative to a participant. An understanding of the kinds of situational irony is largely a recognition of the different ways of being 'outside the situation of the participant'. This is rather different from verbal irony, but we will see at the end of this section that there are some connections.

The participant can be a child, or some other individual who is developmentally or inherently unable to fully understand their situation, while the audience is developmentally more advanced than the participant – an older child, or an adult, for example. An example is Henry James's *What Maisie Knew* (1897). The child Maisie reports events in the adult world without fully understanding them, but we as adults can reintepret her descriptions in the light of our adult understanding of kinds of event; thus we recognize Maisie as 'subject to situational irony'. Situational irony can also separate a child character from a child reader; many children's books expect their readers to recognize that the child character is unable to understand their own situation, and that this understanding relates to their limits as children; the ten-year-old readers of Jacqueline Wilson's *The Suitcase Kid* (1992) are expected to understand more about the ten-year-old character Andrea's situation than she herself can understand; and part of this understanding is that the child reader is – like all readers – always outside the situation of the characters in the book. Thus a reader may be able to overcome the developmental limits associated with a child of their own age, by virtue of the superior position of being a reader. Even very young children's books encourage this: Beatrix Potter's illustrations to *The Tale of Peter Rabbit* (1902) encourage the child to identify to some extent with the animal characters (by putting the child looking at the picture at an eye-height just above that of the rabbits), and to see the rabbits as like the children themselves, while also enabling them to see the rabbits from the outside, permitting the assignment of situational irony. Another kind of 'limited' participant might include someone with a cognitive impairment that prevents them fully understanding their situation; this might include the autistic narrator of Mark Haddon's *The Curious Incident of the Dog in the Night-time* (2003) or the cognitively impaired narrator of book 1 of William Faulkner's *The Sound and the Fury* (1929). Finally, the participant might be non-human, and so unable to understand their situation (in comparison with us, as humans); they might be an alien, or an animal.

These ways of separating the reader from the participant are all ways of Othering the participant: that is, defining the participant not just as different but also as less than us. But these Othered participants can also encourage us to read the situational ironies in reverse, so that we identify with the character in the book as having a special kind of knowledge that we as readers lack; it is as though we temporarily depart from our own culturally contextualized selves to inhabit the fictional characters and then look back at ourselves and thereby subject ourselves to situational irony. Thus a child or animal in a book may by their difference be able to understand our adult human situation in ways that we ourselves cannot understand; now we are caught inside the situational irony and presented as such by the characters in the book. The *Harry Potter* books work in this way, encouraging the child reader to identify with the Othered 'wizards' and to look back at humans as limited and unable to understand the complexities of the world we live in. Similarly, in many novels a 'foreigner' comes to our society and, because of their impaired familiarity with it (which in some ways subjects them to situational irony), they describe our society in ways that show that we also do not fully understand our situation, thus subjecting us to situational irony; an example of this would be George Mikes's *How To Be an Alien* (1946), an Othering description of British society in the 1950s written for a British audience from the perspective of a Hungarian immigrant.

Another way of being outside the situation of a participant is to be historically later than the participant. The historical irony here arises because the participant's understanding of what events mean is contrary to a later, better and fuller understanding of them. Similarly, a participant may have convictions about how events will play out in (their) future, but from our later perspective we know that they will play out very differently.

Dramatic irony can be understood as a sub-kind of situational irony, most prototypically found in the theatre. A character on stage and involved in a dramatic action has a specific belief that the audience knows to be false. Typically, that incorrect belief will be about some crucial component of the plot, and hence the dramatic irony functions as a narrative mechanism:

Pedro: Sure I had dwelt forever on her bosom – But stay, he's here.

[*Enter Belvile dressed in Antonio's clothes.*]

Florinda *(aside)*:   'Tis not Belvile; half my fears are vanished.

In this extract from Aphra Behn's play *The Rover* (1677), Florinda has a belief about an event that is incorrect; the audience, from their vantage point 'outside the situation' of the stage knows that in fact Belville has entered the stage. A writer may use the physical arrangement of the stage – with sightlines accessible to the audience but not to the characters – to distinguish the situations of the characters and the audience and hence to create dramatic irony.

All these examples of situational irony have in common that the irony is created by a difference in situation and knowledge between the participants in events on the one hand and the audience to those events (us) on the other hand. The irony is not created by a person as such, but can be attributed to the events themselves as they occur. (Of course the events themselves might have been created by a playwright or novelist, but this is ignored in thinking of these ironies as having no human 'causer'.) Instead of being attributed to a person, situational irony can be attributed to notions such as fate (in French it is called 'ironie du sort' – irony of fate), or time, or history, or life (as in 'life's little ironies'), or circumstances, or indeed anything: the first quote in the *OED* for this meaning of irony refers to 'the irony of war' (that it is better to fire an arrow at the horse than at the rider).

1.3 Mechanisms of irony

What makes verbal irony different from lying? A person who speaks or writes communicates both a proposition and his or her attitude towards that proposition. In both verbal irony and lying, the communicator has an attitude of disbelief towards the proposition. In verbal irony that attitude of disbelief is made clear (by various signals), while in lying the disbelief is concealed. For irony to be successful, the audience/readership must be able to recognize that there is a true attitude of disbelief towards a proposition expressed by the text. In principle, any kind of evidence might be used to indicate that there is a true attitude of disbelief towards the proposition; in this section we briefly consider some of the more common kinds of evidence.

One kind of evidence involves a contradiction between what the text tells us and what we already know. Unless there is good reason to abandon our previous beliefs, we will therefore adopt an attitude of disbelief towards the text. This is not enough on its own to give rise to irony, though: on its own, this might just generate a decision that the author has made a mistake. Thus we must be convinced that the author also shares the beliefs that we brought to the text. A second kind of evidence for irony comes from exaggeration and overemphasis, including hyperbole, emphatic (insincere) statements of belief, extensive use of superlatives, or exaggerations in speaking (as in typical sarcasm). Overemphasis functions to communicate the irony in the quote from Jane Austen with which we began.

Overstatement is an instance of a more general way in which a text signals the presence of irony, which is by some kind of disruption. In most texts it is possible to distinguish the normal characteristics of the text from the disruptive characteristics. In a rhyming poem, the rhymes are the default case and any failure to rhyme would be disruptive; in prose, a rhyme would be disruptive where rhyme is not expected. (The terms 'unmarked' and 'marked' are sometimes used to characterize the normal and disruptive elements of the text, respectively). Looking for disruptions in a text is always a useful way of entering into and beginning to understand the workings of a text, and the manipulation of disruptions can be a powerful communicative tool. To indicate the presence of irony, the text can be disrupted in various ways. Internal inconsistency is one kind of disruption that is fairly characteristic of irony. A common example of this second type is where the register of the text changes unexpectedly; in this case, we say that the voice of the text is inconsistent. In Henry Reed's poem 'Naming of Parts' (1946), there are at least two registers: some of the lines are spoken as if by a military instructor and some as if by a dreamy romantic. Yet there is no explicit change of speaker. In this case, the irony comes from the fact that the two registers express different attitudes that contradict one another and yet the whole poem seems to come from a single source; thus one attitude must be false.

1.4 Uncertain ironies

Irony is sometimes clear, but sometimes we feel that a writer or speaker is communicating propositions that we think they are unlikely to believe, but we do not have clear evidence either to think that they are being ironic or that they are lying. Problems in identifying or interpreting irony can arise when author and reader are separated by major differences in what they know – if, for example, they are separated by major differences in time or place or culture. Because one of the ways of marking irony is for the text to contradict what we already know, the identification of irony can depend on our (culturally dependent) knowledge. In some cases, the fact that cultural or subcultural differences can be a barrier to irony can be exploited by an author. Dick Hebdige once proposed that the new wave song 'Heart of Glass' by Blondie is capable of being read ironically (given a certain subcultural 'punk' awareness) or non-ironically (in mainstream culture), thus maximizing its audience. Perhaps the barriers to cross-cultural interpretation of irony explain the claim that is sometimes made that people in a certain foreign culture 'lack the capacity for irony', because irony is difficult to recognize across cultures given its dependence on culturally dependent knowledge. Nevertheless, given that irony is an exploitation of some very basic characteristics of human communication, irony should be possible in every language and every culture, even if outsiders have difficulty in identifying or interpreting it.

The difficulties just mentioned are the consequence – often accidental – of cultural difference. But difficulties in the identification or interpretation of irony can also be built into the workings of a text. Thus it is possible to find texts that are apparently ironic (e.g. what is said contradicts what we know), where there is a narrator, but where it is difficult to judge whether the narrator is the victim of a structural irony (i.e. a naive narrator, unaware of the ironies) or whether instead the narrator is to be understood as producing verbal irony (and hence is aware of the irony); Samuel Beckett's fiction and plays often present a problem of this kind. Similarly, texts might have overt ironies where there are two opposing voices within them, each taking different attitudes towards a proposition, but where it is difficult to decide which of the two voices is the voice of truth. These problems are characteristically found in modernist texts, where there may be many competing voices.

As an illustration of some of the more complex possibilities of irony, consider part of Shelley's poem 'Ozymandias' (1819). This is a poem that – we assume deliberately – generates a number of un-resolvable interpretive problems, among which is the identification and attribution of the irony in the, inscription cited in lines 10–11:

9 And on the pedestal these words appear:
10 'My name is Ozymandias, king of kings:
11 Look on my works, ye Mighty, and despair!'

The inscription is found on a pedestal, surrounded by fragments of a statue and otherwise 'nothing besides remains' in the desert where it stands. If the inscription is to be interpreted as 'Despair because even my great works will come to nothing' then it is not ironic at all; it is correctly believed by all parties concerned. If alternatively the inscription is to be interpreted as 'Despair because my works are so great' then this proposition is falsely believed by Ozymandias, and correctly disbelieved by us (because the works have now vanished over the course of time). However, even if we identify the text as ironic, there is still a problem of attribution, because it is not clear what attitude is taken by the sculptor – the person who has written these words on the statute: did the sculptor believe or disbelieve the proposition 'Despair because my works are so great'? It is not clear that these questions can be answered: whether there is an irony, and how exactly the attitudes are to be attributed. These uncertainties are characteristic of Shelley's work in general, and in particular of this poem, which is rich in uncertainties.

1.5 Why use irony?

It is possible for us to say something that we do not believe to be true, and by so doing to communicate a rich range of meanings that we *do* believe to be true. This is the basis for verbal irony as a communicative practice.

Irony might, for example, be used to express a particular world view that we can never really be certain in our knowledge and beliefs. Even the simplest and most straightforward ironies (as in the Austen text cited earlier) demonstrate the existence of incorrect certainties; and more complex ironies such as those found in Shelley's poem can create a sense of the impossibility of being certain of anything.

While irony can destabilize, it can also have stabilizing functions. Thus Austen uses irony to confirm the authority of a particular voice (the narrator's own voice) as the voice of truth. Furthermore, because irony requires the reader to bring a certain kind of background knowledge to the text in order to make sense of it, irony can require the reader to make certain assumptions in order to interpret the text: in order to understand Austen's first sentence we are forced to take on a set of attitudes towards women, men, marriage and society, which the novel will then manipulate.

ACTIVITY 1.1

This is the beginning of H.G. Wells's novel *The War of the Worlds* (1898) (note the date):

No one would have believed in the last years of the nineteenth century that this world was being watched keenly and closely by intelligences greater than man's and yet as mortal as his own; that as men busied themselves about their various concerns they were scrutinised and studied, perhaps almost as narrowly as a man with a microscope might scrutinise the transient creatures that swarm and multiply in a drop of water. With infinite complacency men went to and fro over this globe about their little affairs, serene in their assurance of their empire over matter. It is possible that the infusoria under the microscope do the same. No one gave a thought to the older worlds of space as sources of human danger, or thought of them only to dismiss the idea of life upon them as impossible or improbable. It is curious to recall some of the mental habits of those departed days. At most terrestrial men fancied there might be other men upon Mars, perhaps inferior to themselves and ready to welcome a missionary enterprise. Yet across the gulf of space, minds that are to our minds as ours are to those of the beasts that perish, intellects vast and cool and unsympathetic, regarded this earth with envious eyes, and slowly and surely drew their plans against us. And early in the twentieth century came the great disillusionment.

The planet Mars, I scarcely need remind the reader, revolves about the sun at a mean distance of 140,000,000 miles, and the light and heat it receives from the sun is barely half of that received by this world. It must be, if the nebular hypothesis has any truth, older than our world; and long before this earth ceased to be molten, life upon its surface must have begun its course. The fact that it is scarcely one seventh of the volume of the earth must have accelerated its cooling to the temperature at which life could begin. It has air and water and all that is necessary for the support of animated existence.

Yet so vain is man, and so blinded by his vanity, that no writer, up to the very end of the nineteenth century, expressed any idea that intelligent life might have developed there far, or indeed at all, beyond its earthly level. Nor was it generally understood that since Mars is older than our earth, with scarcely a quarter of the superficial area and remoter from the sun, it necessarily follows that it is not only more distant from time's beginning but nearer its end.

1 Explain why we might say that Wells develops 'situational irony' in this passage.
2 Are there examples also of verbal irony? If so, does the verbal irony interact with the situational irony?
3 What evidence does Wells offer the reader that the text is ironic.
4 Who is being 'Othered' in this passage.
5 What purposes might the irony serve? If you know anything about science fiction more generally, discuss some of the ways in which Wells's use of irony is here typical of the genre.

Reading

Fabb, N. (1997) *Linguistics and Literature*, Oxford: Blackwell, Chapter 10.

Furniss, T.E. and Bath, M. (1996) *Reading Poetry*, London: Longman, Chapter 8.

Leech, G. and Short, M. (1981) *Style in Fiction*, London: Longman, pp. 277–80.

MacCabe, C. (1979) *James Joyce and the Revolution of the Word*, London: Macmillan.

Muecke, D.C. (1970) *Irony and the Ironic*, London: Methuen.

Sperber, D. and Wilson, D. (1995) *Relevance: Communication and Cognition*, Oxford: Blackwell, Chapter 4.

Unit 2

Narrative

In this unit we examine narrative. Narratives are stories involving a sequence of related events. There are various kinds of relationship between events in a narrative. The most obvious kind is where one event causes another. Such causal connections link one event with another and function partly to give unity to the narrative, and partly to enable the narrative to draw moral conclusions about the consequences of actions.

In the simplest narrative texts, there is a single series of events with causal connections between them. More complex narrative texts might be compounded from simple narratives, with two or more simultaneous narratives (perhaps as plot and sub-plot), or with narratives in sequence that are only loosely connected, perhaps through sharing the same basic character (this is the structure of picaresque narratives).

2.1 Narrative form and narrative content

Much thinking about narrative distinguishes between two dimensions or layers of interest, which we will call 'narrative form' and 'narrative content'. The content of a narrative is a collection of represented events, along with the participants in those events, and the circumstances of those events. The form of a narrative is the way in which those events are represented through a particular narrative medium (usually spoken or written language, and/or images). Many components of a narrative show a tension between content and form, as we shall see in this unit.

The distinction between content and form is realized in different ways for different aspects of narrative. If we consider narrative events, we can distinguish between the content order of events and the form order of events. The 'content order' is the chronological order of events (events in the sequence in which they supposedly 're- ally' occurred). The 'form order' is the order in which the narrative presents these events to us. In the simplest narratives, the presentational or form order is the same as chronological or content order: thus form order = content order. In fact, if there is nothing to tell us otherwise, we just assume that the orders are the same and hence that, if we are told first one thing and then another, the first thing we heard about happened first and the second thing happened second. Thus, if a narrative simply states:

The queen died. The king died.

we typically assume that the queen died before the king and that probably the latter's death was a result of the former. However, it is also possible for narratives to present events out of chronological sequence. For instance:

The king died. Only a month earlier the queen had died in child birth.

The presentation of events (the order in which they are narrated) does not match their chronological occurrence. There is thus a mismatch between form order and content order, with content being reordered. Complex narratives, such as we find in film or the novel, often tend to manipulate the presentation of events. Detective fiction, for instance, may begin with the crime and spend the rest of the narrative uncovering the chain of events behind it. Flashbacks in film also manipulate form order and content order. Thus, for example, the film *Sunset Boulevard* (1950) begins with a body floating in a pool; the next images we see represent events that occurred earlier than the first image of the body in the pool.

There are various terms used to describe the distinction between form order and content order in a narrative; one terminological distinction is between 'story' (= the content order of events, the order in which they supposedly happened) and 'discourse' (= the form order of events, the order in which they are presented to us in the narrative as it is told.)

A mismatch between content order and form order is an example of an 'aesthetic strategy', a strategy that might typically be used in creating an aesthetic object such as a novel, film, oral narrative, etc. It is never possible to pin down a single function for an aesthetic strategy; instead; it might perform any one of a number of functions. The strategy of mismatching content order and form order might be used to create enigmas (we are told the consequences before we are told how they were achieved), to create suspense (the order of events is interrupted by a flashback), to help organize our understanding of the content (crucial background history is delayed until we need to be told it) and so on. The Russian Formalists, a group of theorists working in the early twentieth century, focused their energies on an attempt to establish what makes a text 'literary'; one basic idea was that a text is literary to the extent that our attention is drawn to its aesthetic strategies. One very noticeable aesthetic strategy is a mismatch between form order (which they termed *sjuzhet* – something like 'story' above) and content order (which they called *fabula*, something like 'discourse' above); hence such a mismatch helps define a text as literary.

A mismatch between form and content can have consequences for narrative pace. Minor events in the narrative can be dwelt on at length and major events treated briefly or compressed. Spelling out minor events in detail can give the effect of slowing down – retarding – the narrative. Conversely, condensed treatment of a crucial event seems to speed the narrative up.

Orwell's account of an execution in Burma ('A Hanging', 1931) deals with events that last only about half an hour. The prisoner is picked up at eight and is pronounced dead by eight minutes past eight. Orwell's account, however, dwells in detail on small events that retard the progress to the execution: a dog runs out to interrupt the procession; the prisoner steps aside to avoid a puddle; his final prayer seems to last for ever.

Here is how Orwell dwells on one of these moments that retard the narrative:

> And once, in spite of the men who gripped him by each shoulder, he stepped slightly aside to avoid a puddle on the path.
>
> It is curious, but till that moment I had never realized what it means to destroy a healthy, conscious man. When I saw the prisoner step aside to avoid the puddle, I saw the mystery, the unspeakable wrongness, of cutting a life short when it is in full tide. This man was not dying, he was alive just as we were alive. All the organs of his body were working – bowels digesting food, skin renewing itself, nails growing, tissues forming – all toiling away in solemn foolery. His nails would still be growing when he stood on the drop, when he was falling through the air with a tenth of a second to live. His eyes saw the yellow gravel and the grey walls, and his brain still remembered, foresaw, reasoned – reasoned even about puddles. He and we were a party of men walking together, seeing, hearing, feeling, understanding the same world; and in two minutes, with a sudden snap, one of us would be gone – one mind less, one world less.

But when the end finally comes, it comes swiftly:

> Suddenly the superintendent made up his mind. Throwing up his head he made a swift motion with his stick. 'Chalo!' he shouted almost fiercely.
>
> There was a clanking noise, and then dead silence. The prisoner had vanished, and the rope was twisting on itself.

So, just as dwelling on some events can slow the narrative down, compressing major events can give the impression of acceleration. We get the effect of the narrative decelerating when things are described very slowly (an effect also seen in slow motion sections of films); and narratives can also accelerate or jump when two events separated in the narrative content by major gaps in time are placed next to each other. A strategy of this kind is used by Woolf in *To the Lighthouse* (1927). Various functions are possible for this aesthetic strategy, which again exploits the difference between narrative form and narrative content.

'Narrative coherence' amounts to our recognition that we are being told one unified story – which means that we understand why we are told every event, we understand how events fit together, and, if there are any sub-stories inside the main story, these sub-stories make sense in terms of the overall story, perhaps as commenting on it (e.g. sub-plots in a Shakespeare play or a story one character tells another). An interesting test for coherence in a narrative is to try formulating the narrative as a whole as a single sentence, or even as a single word; this exercise can bring out quite abstract kinds of coherence (the title might carry out this function). Even the author of the narrative may not always find this easy to do. F. Scott Fitzgerald went through a series of titles for his most famous novel, including *Among the Ash-Heaps and Millionaires, Trimalchio in West Egg, Trimalchio* and *The Golden-Hatted Gatsby,* before finally settling for *The Great Gatsby* (1925). In retrospect, his final choice seems to capture the core meaning of the novel in ways eluded by the earlier attempts. One of the distinctions between form and content in a narrative is that form is inherently more coherent than content. If we take narrative content to be analogous to the way reality is, then we acknowledge its complexity, density and multiplicity; reality is a mess rather than a single coherent thing, and narrative content takes on this implied messiness. In contrast, the organization of narrative content by selection and ordering, which is part of the construction of narrative form, is the creation of order, a fitting together, a making sense, and in general a creation of coherence. Narratives tend to move from a lack to a resolution, a particular kind of beginning to a particular kind of end, but these are formal characteristics that give the narrative its coherence; the implied reality represented by the narrative (the narrative content) lacks any coherent movement from a particular kind of beginning to a particular kind of end – this is imposed upon it by the process of narration.

Finally, another possible kind of mismatch between narrative form and narrative content comes when we consider 'narrative point of view' (see **Unit 3**). Events in narrative content just occur; they do not occur from a particular point of view. However, in a particular narrative, the selection of events and the way in which they are described will interact with the choice of a focalizer from whose perspective the events are described. In Henry James's classic ghost story, *The Turn of the Screw* (1898), crucial events are presented to us from the perspective of the governess. From her perspective the children in her charge are in danger of demonic possession from ghostly apparitions; but readers may wonder if the apparitions are merely figments of the governess's neurotic imagination. It is difficult to decide what actually happens in the narrative because of the overriding position given to the governess's point of view. In *The Turn of the Screw* the point of view is that of a character who is supposedly involved in the events (and hence has a particular angle on them). In other cases the narrator stands outside the events of the story.

The use of a narrator is thus an aesthetic strategy, which, like all such strategies, can be used in various ways and for various purposes. Point of view might be switched in the course of the narrative (a technique systematically used by the author Philip K. Dick, or in the film *Rashomon* (1951) for example); the consequence might be, again, that we become uncertain about the narrative content because it alters depending on point of view. Also, because narrators are fictional constructions, it is possible to invent narrators who are fantastic in various ways; so an animal may be a narrator, or a dead person (the body in the pool in *Sunset Boulevard* is also its narrator).

In this section we have seen that differences between narrative form and narrative content can be exploited in aesthetic strategies. In some cases, the narrative form is rigidly constrained but variation is possible in narrative content as in flashbacks, while in other cases it is the content that is constrained and the form that is unconstrained as in narrative pace acceleration and deceleration. In other cases, the narrative content simply lacks a characteristic that can be found in narrative form, such as narrative coherence and narrative point of view. In the next section we look at how events themselves, and the participants in those events, also show a tension between narrative form and narrative content.

2.2 The typicality of characters and events

The raw material of narrative consists of events with their accompanying actors and circumstances. These, we have suggested, comprise the basic content of a narrative, which becomes shaped into form by ordering and reordering their sequence and by the choice of point of view. However, one of the characteristics of narratives is that the events themselves are often stereotyped, with the genre of the narrative to some extent requiring certain kinds of typical event – a marriage, a murder, a chase, a disguise uncovered, a false accusation, etc. The very typicality of events moves them from the level of narrative content to the level of narrative form – they are among the components from which a narrative form is built. Hence, there is a conflict for events between the tendency towards typicality (a formal characteristic) and the demands for the individuality, uniqueness and realism that are associated with narrative content. A marriage in a narrative is (supposedly) a specific marriage, which really happens in all its complex and individual details in the fictional world; but, at the same time, it is a typical event with all its individuality stripped off – a building block of the narrative, perhaps as one of the components that helps end the narrative. Typical events in a narrative are called motifs. Folklorists catalogue motifs in folktales (naming and numbering them, tracing their occurrence across storytelling history).

Just as events in a narrative are both individuated and typical, so also characters in a narrative are both individual and typical.

On the one hand, characters are representative of supposedly real people in the fictional world represented by the narrative. On the other hand, characters can also be seen as parts of the mechanism that drives the narrative from beginning to end; in this sense they can be labelled depending on their function in the narrative (this is the characters as elements of narrative form). This approach is particularly associated with Vladimir Propp, who suggested that typical characters in Russian fairy tales perform typical functions. Propp identifies a character function on the basis of the character's involvement in specific types of event; for example, for Propp, the 'hero' is the character function of the character who, in the fairy tales under discussion:

- is forbidden to do something;
- is sent off to resolve a lack;
- acquires a magical object;
- fights the villain;
- is marked (e.g. injured, or given something like a ring);
- is pursued;
- arrives somewhere unrecognized;
- is married and ascends the throne.

Propp lists seven character-functions, not all of which are clearly useful in all narratives. However, one in particular, 'the donor', does appear to be found in many kinds of narrative. One specific character is often particularly important in enabling a narrative to move from lack to fulfilment. Donor (= giver) is the name given to this character, and typically the donor(-function) will give the hero(-function) some object that enables the hero to conclude the narrative by restoring the lack. In Propp's fairy tales the gift is often magical (a cloak of invisibility, or a special weapon), but if we move beyond fairy tales to more realistic narratives we still find that there may be something magical about the gift (e.g. it may function unexpectedly, like a Bible carried in a shirt pocket that deflects a bullet). A typical type of donor is an old person who gives the hero(-function) something in exchange for a favour. Sometimes the gift is simply information (as when the dying character in a thriller gasps out crucial information with his or her last breath).

When we seek Propp's character functions in more realistic texts, we may need to adapt them in this manner, interpreting the name of the character function rather abstractly. Thus 'the princess' is just the character who is sought for by the hero, possibly because that character has been snatched by a villain. This means that the princess might for example be a kidnapped young boy; if the only family member otherwise involved is the boy's mother then she might be classified as 'the father of the princess'. This is the power of Propp's approach: it enables us to understand the characters functionally in terms of their role in the narrative rather than just realistically in terms of their identity.

Narratives permeate culture as a way of making sense, packaging experience in particular ways for particular groups and audiences. Thus, as part of the self-representations and imaginings of a culture, an individual can be classified on the basis of some characteristic – race, ethnic group, gender, age, sexuality, size, skin colour, etc. It is interesting to look at the relationship between a particular classificatory characteristic of a character and the function played by that character in the narrative. For example, in many contemporary American films an African-American character has the function of donor. The donor typically has a minimal presence in the narrative (usually appearing briefly) but has a crucial role in enabling it to develop and come to a conclusion. In any particular film, we could interpret the use of an African-American donor as making a historical claim: that African-Americans function as donor for the development of the 'narrative' of the US economy. Or we could interpret it in terms of a contradictory position taken by the film with regard to racism, since it enables racial discrimination at the level of employment (the actor gets a small part) while carrying a positive message at the level of – meaning (without this African-American character the narrative could not be resolved).

2.3 The narrative arc: from lack to resolution

Narratives are typically about change. We can think of a change like this:

situation A   changes to   situation B

The changes are often brought about by human actions, and the notion that actions are causes that have effects is an important part of many narratives. Often in a narrative the changes that take place – particularly the important ones – can be understood in terms of situation A being a lack or disruption, which is restored or resolved by situation B. So we can think of many narratives as having arcs like this:

situation A   changes to   situation B

lack   leads to   restoration

The lack may occur when a family member leaves home; this lack may be restored when a family is reunited at the end (it need not be exactly the same people; the crucial point is that a lacking family is replaced by a restored family). Or the lack may be the theft of an object, which is hunted and finally recovered. The lack may be a personal lack; the hero or heroine may begin in ignorance and end in wisdom, or begin in isolation and end in community. There are many other variations on the pattern of lack and restoration, and the movement from one to the other is often the driving force of a narrative.

   One very important aspect related to the unity and coherence of a narrative is its achievement of 'closure'. Closure is the 'tying up' of the narrative, whereby loose ends are dealt with, problems solved and questions answered. The restoration of a lack is a form of closure. Few narratives are completely without closure (if they are, we think of them as experimental or avant-garde), though, because most narratives involve plenty of lacks and plenty of restorations, there is typically some lack of closure – a few issues (though not usually central ones) may not be resolved. Sometimes the narrative ends with closure but at the very end of the text a new lack may open up again; the text in its conclusion opens up a new narrative (perhaps leading to a new text – a sequel – that will bring closure to the lack that begins the new narrative). The existence or non-existence of closure often reveals a moral or ideological position. For example, if a narrative can be closed by the major male and female characters getting married, the narrative potentially carries a message about the virtues of marriage. Along similar lines, we could look at what constitutes or causes a 'lack' or a disruption in the terms of a particular narrative: if the absence of the father at the beginning of a film constitutes its initial lack, then the narrative can be read to mean that nuclear families should stay together.

We can exemplify some of these points by looking at some aspects of the narrative of N. Scott Momaday's novel *House Made of Dawn* (1966), about a young American Indian man after the Second World War and his relationship with his culture; as in many narratives, the novel is concerned with an interior change in the hero from lack to fulfilment (in this case the change is emphasized by the fact that the narrative is constructed to parallel an all-night healing ceremony). The novel is divided up into a one-page prologue and four numbered sections. The prologue is echoed in the last page of the novel in that both parts describe a runner (the hero); they are somewhat distinct from the development of events in the narrative, and we could call one the 'orientation' and the other the 'coda' (see next section). After the orientation, the narrative begins with the return home of the hero from the war; we can interpret this as an inversion of the common opening in which the hero leaves home. Normally leaving home is seen as disruptive, but in this novel the hero is unable to fit into the home that he returns to, and so his *return* is the creation of a lack or a disruption. At the end of the novel, the hero walks out of the village, so providing a mirror-image of the beginning. However, he is now integrated into the culture. In the prologue (the orientation) he runs alone; at the end he runs with others. These lacks and closures are to do with movement between the village and the surrounding landscape (a culture–nature opposition); the closure of the novel involves the unifying of the two, a unity expressed in the title *House Made of Dawn*.

2.4 How narratives begin and end

We have looked at ways in which narrative form is a management of the narrative content it represents. We now consider some of the ways in which the narrative form is a response to the context of narration, and in particular how narratives are started and finished. We can call the movement from lack to resolution the 'narrative proper'. The text of the narrative may begin before the lack is revealed, and may end some time after the lack is resolved. This extra material functions to lead into and out of the narrative proper. The hearer or reader must enter into a narrative, and must then exit from the narrative at the end, and there are characteristic strategies for achieving this entry and exit; we first consider some 'entry strategies' and then some 'exit strategies'.

Entry strategies include the title of the narrative and material quoted from elsewhere (an epigraph); these may function to set the leading idea of the narrative – the single notion that gives the narrative coherence. There may occasionally be an initial 'abstract', which is a summary of what is to come. Very often, the text begins by setting the scene; this is called the 'orientation' of the narrative, and may include a representation of the place where the narrative is to take place and perhaps some initial details about the characters. Orientations can be stereotyped; fairy tales may begin with a stereotyped orientation 'Once upon a time there was . . .', and many films begin with the camera travelling over a city towards a particular locality.

Exit strategies are ways of ending the text once the lack has been resolved. This material is generally called the 'coda'; it can contain elements that mirror the 'abstract' (e.g. a final summary) or the 'orientation' (by describing some kind of departure from the scene). It can also be stereotyped, as in the fairy-tale coda 'And they all lived happily ever after . . .'. Codas sometimes fill a historical gap between an explicitly historical narrative content and now, the time of narrating and reading/hearing; thus a film might end by telling us what happened to various characters between the end of the narrative proper and now.

ACTIVITY 2.1

1 Choose a nineteenth-century novel. You will need to read* the novel for this exercise.

2 Why does the novel have this particular title? In answering this, consider (a) whether the title is an aid in the interpretation of the novel, (b) whether it creates initial expectations that are important for the reading of the novel, and (c) whether it has this title for marketing reasons.

3 Outline the structure of the beginning of the novel, distinguishing the following components (if they exist), or any other components you think are relevant: title, prologue or abstract (introducing a text in an author's voice, perhaps summarizing some of what is to come); epigraph (= a quotation); orientation, beginning of the narrative proper, etc.

---

* This activity can be understood in part as asking you to read different parts of a novel in different ways – a useful skill. Approaches to reading sometimes distinguish (1) close reading: reading every word carefully; (2) skimming: reading quickly through a whole text in order to get a sense of the whole, skipping chunks that you judge to be less crucial to your needs; or (3) scanning: reading quickly while looking for particular things in the text. This exercise asks you to read closely the beginning and the end of the novel, while requiring you to skim the rest (so that you have a sense of the structure of the rest of the novel, while paying relatively little attention to detail).

3.1 Comment on any continuities or blurred boundaries between these components.

3.2 If any of these components are absent, and you think there is some interest in their absence, comment on it.

(You will need to make your own decision about how far into the novel the 'beginning' extends.)

4 Does the ending of the novel relate in any ways to the beginning of the novel? Describe all the links you can find (e.g. you might expect a restoration at the end of lacks that were indicated at the beginning, and you might also find certain kinds of 'return' to the situation described at the beginning).

Reading

Briggs, K. (1970) *A Dictionary of British Folk Tales in the English Language*, London: Routledge & Kegan Paul.

Fabb, N. (1997) *Linguistics and Literature*, Oxford: Blackwell, Chapters 7–8.

Finnegan, R. (1992) *Oral Traditions and the Verbal Arts: A Guide to Research Practices*, London: Routledge.

Murray, J.H. (1997) *Hamlet on the Holodeck: The Future of Narrative in Cyberspace*, Cambridge, MA: MIT Press.

Onega Jaén, S. and Garcia Landa, J.A. (eds) (1996) *Narratology: An Introduction*, London: Longman.

Propp, Vladimir (1968) *Morphology of the Folktale*, Austin, TX: University of Texas Press.

Toolan, M. (2001) *Narrative: A Critical Linguistic Introduction*, 2nd edn, London: Routledge.

Narrative Point of View

3.1 'Story' and 'narration'

In most theories of narrative two main dimensions or levels are identified. The first consists of the basic events or actions, in the chronological order in which they are supposed to have happened, together with the circumstances in which the actions are performed. This level is sometimes referred to as the 'story'. The second level includes the techniques and devices used for telling the story to the reader. This latter level is sometimes referred to as 'discourse' (see **Unit 2, Narrative**) but also as 'narration'. In effect, these two levels may be seen as corresponding to the distinction between the tale itself and the manner in which it is told – a distinction that is based upon our intuitive recognition that the same tale can be told in different ways.

3.2 Point of view and narration

The term 'point of view' in the discussion of prose fiction has been used in a variety of ways (see Fowler, 1986; Simpson, 1993, 2004). It can be used literally to refer to visual perspective – the spatial position and angle of vision from which a scene is presented. It can also be used, metaphorically, to designate the ideological framework and presuppositions of a text (e.g. 'the point of view of the emergent bourgeoisie', or 'a male perspective'). Finally, it can be used as a term for describing and analysing distinctions between types of narration – the different types of relation of the teller to the tale in any narrative.

It is this relationship – between point of view and narration – that will be examined in this unit.

The simplest distinction that we can make in discussing point of view is between two types of narration – a first person 'I-narration' and a third person 'they-narration'. Thus, if we take a narrative event such as 'the end of a relationship', the same event could be narrated in at least two ways:

She texted him that it was all over (third person).

Or:

I texted him that it was all over (first person).

The terminology, first person versus third person, is based upon the grammatical distinction between three persons. In describing the grammar of the personal pronoun system in English (I, you, he, she, it, we, you, they), items that refer to, or include, the speaker (I, we) are termed 'first person'. Items that refer to the addressee (you) are termed 'second person'. Items that refer to anyone or anything other than the speaker and the addressee are termed 'third person'.

Given the options in the pronoun system, we might wonder if second person narration ever occurs. In fact, although it is extremely rare, some examples do exist – the best known being perhaps Italo Calvino's *If on a Winter's Night a Traveller* (1981). The reason why second person narration is so rare relates to the ease with which both first person and third person reference can be restricted to figures in a narrative and the converse difficulty in making the second person refer only to a figure in the tale: the second person always somehow points to, or constructs for itself, an addressee. Thus:

You texted him that it was all over,

sounds like a question to a co-conversationalist rather than a description of a narrative event. Accordingly, we will deal only with features of first versus third person narration.

3.2.1 First person narration

First person narration may be found in a wide range of novels otherwise different in style and period. Novels such as Daniel Defoe's *Robinson Crusoe* (1719), James Hogg's *The Private Memoirs and Confessions of a Justified Sinner* (1824), Charlotte Brontë's *Jane Eyre* (1847), Mark Twain's *Huckleberry Finn* (1884), Philip Roth's *Portnoy's Complaint* (1967) and Alice Walker's *The Color Purple* (1983) are all told in the first person. Indeed, in the case of Robinson Crusoe, the very chapter headings emphasize the use of the first person: 'I Go to Sea', 'I Am Very Ill and Frighted', 'I Sow My Grain', 'I Am Very Seldom Idle'. In this example, and in most of those listed above, the I-narrator is also the central protagonist of the tale, so that the person central to the action of the story is also telling it.

For example, the 'Private Memoirs and Confessions of a Sinner' (which is the central narrative of *The Private Memoirs and Confessions of a Justified Sinner*, framed before and after by 'The Editor's Narrative', also narrated in the first person) begins as follows:

> My life has been a life of trouble and turmoil; of change and vicissitude; of anger and exultation; of sorrow and of vengeance. My sorrows have all been for a slighted gospel, and my vengeance has been wreaked on its adversaries. Therefore in the might of heaven I will sit down and write . . . I was born an outcast in the world, in which I was destined to act so conspicuous a part.

It concludes with the impending death of the sinner and a series of farewells:

> Farewell, world, with all thy miseries; for comforts and joys hast thou none! Farewell, woman, whom I have despised and shunned; and man whom I have hated; whom, nevertheless, I desire to leave in charity! And thou, sun, bright emblem of a brighter effulgence, I bid farewell to thee also! I do not now take my last look of thee, for to thy glorious orb shall a poor

suicide's last earthly look be raised. But, ah! Who is yon that I see approaching furiously – his stern face blackened with horrid despair! My hour is at hand. – Almighty God, what is this that I am about to do! The hour of repentance is past, and now my fate is inevitable – *Amen for ever!* I will now seal up my little book, and conceal it; and cursed be he who trieth to alter or amend!

Thus, in the 'Private Memoirs and Confessions of a Sinner' the sinner's life is coterminous with the narrative, which is told by him in the first person as the very figure who acts 'so conspicuous a part' in the tale.

First person narration, however, can be used in a quite different way where the story is told not by the central protagonist but by a subsidiary character. Indeed, the 'Private Memoirs and Confessions of a Sinner' is framed – as we have said – by just such a first person narration, purportedly that of the editor and discoverer of the 'confessions' narrative that the sinner had completed just before his death.

F. Scott Fitzgerald's *The Great Gatsby* (1922) is a well-known case of the tale being told through the first person narration of a subsidiary character. Although Nick, the narrator, tells the story in the first person, he remains on the margins of the main events, which involve the central figure – Jay Gatsby himself – whose story is thus told from some degree of narrative distance. Here, for instance, is Nick describing Gatsby and Daisy, whose reunion he has helped – almost unwittingly – to make possible:

As I went over to say goodbye I saw that the expression of bewilderment had come back into Gatsby's face, as though a faint doubt had occurred to him as to the quality of his present happiness. Almost five years! There must have been moments even that afternoon when Daisy tumbled short of his dreams – not through her own fault, but because of the colossal vitality of his illusion. It had gone beyond her, beyond everything. He had thrown himself into it with a creative passion, adding to it all the time, decking it out with every bright feather that drifted his way. No amount of fire or freshness can challenge what a man can store up in his ghostly heart.

As I watched him he adjusted himself a little, visibly. His hand took hold of hers, and as she said something low in his ear he turned toward her with a rush of emotion. I think that voice held him most, with its fluctuating feverish warmth, because it couldn't be overdreamed – that voice was a deathless song.

They had forgotten me, but Daisy glanced up and held out her hand; Gatsby didn't know me at all. I looked once more at them and they looked back at me, remotely, possessed by intense life. Then I went out of the room and down the marble steps into the rain, leaving them there together.

Nick's narration does contain some confident, almost poetic, assertions – usually about life: for instance, 'No amount of fire or freshness can challenge what a man can store up in his ghostly heart'; or 'that voice was a deathless song'. However, it is also full of circumspect observation ('I saw that . . .', 'As I watched him . . .', 'I looked once more at them . . .'), where the truth of the events that are described is not certain: 'I saw that the expression of bewilderment had come back into Gatsby's face, *as though a faint doubt* had occurred to him'; or 'There *must have been* moments'; or 'and as *she said something low* in his ear he turned toward her with a rush of emotion'; or '*I think* that voice held him most'. Indeed, the two deaths that separately constitute the spring of the tragedy and its dénouement each happen, so to speak, 'off camera' since Nick is present at neither event.

First person narration, therefore, usually has in-built restrictions, especially when told from the viewpoint of a minor character, though even a central character will be ignorant about some of the things happening around him or her. Whatever its restrictions, however, it projects the reader clearly inside the consciousness of someone in the story giving us the events from a defined observer's position.

3.2.2 Third person narration

Third person narration, by contrast, can be used in such a way that we are not particularly aware of the role of the narrator, who remains outside the action of the tale. In such writing the narration seems to operate as a simple window on the events of the story; and, because the role of the narrator is carefully effaced, this mode of narration acquires a reputation for impersonal, but all-seeing, objectivity. The opening of William Goldings's *Lord of the Flies* (1954) is of this type, in the way it introduces an unnamed boy, who is presented from the outside:

> The boy with fair hair lowered himself down the last few feet of rock and began to pick his way towards the lagoon. Though he had taken off his school sweater and trailed it now from one hand, his grey shirt stuck to him and his hair was plastered to his forehead.

As third rather than first person narration this presents quite different opportunities for readers to align themselves with the story. 'The boy with fair hair' is clearly presented to us at this moment as if observed from without. Indeed, it would be hard to re-cast any of this into first person from the boy's perspective: for instance 'my hair was plastered to my forehead' sounds odd precisely because the boy would simultaneously have to be the subjective agent of the narration and object of its scrutiny. He'd have to be looking at himself.

The opening passage of the novel continues (still in the third person) as follows:

> All round him the long scar smashed into the jungle was a bath of heat. He was clambering heavily among the creepers and broken trunks when a bird, a vision of red and yellow, flashed upwards with a witch-like cry; and this cry was echoed by another.

Although the narration remains in the third person, the sensations described shift to being – in part at least – those of the boy. It could be the boy who feels the long scar in the jungle as a bath of heat and who sees the red and yellow of the bird and who hears its 'witch-like cry'. Indeed, these sentences do not sound as odd as the earlier part of the passage if transformed into the boy's first person narration: for instance, 'All round me the long scar smashed into the jungle was a bath of heat' reads quite appropriately.

In this respect, third person narration is potentially more flexible and enjoys a technical advantage over first person narration. First person narrators have to provide a warrant for knowing the details that they narrate. However, if the narrator is not defined and named, operating instead anonymously in the third person, the narrative does not have to provide a warrant for presenting everything and anything that is going on in the story, whether it is inside the mind of a character or not.

Moreover, it is important to recognize that there are contrasting possibilities within third person narration, which we may sum up in terms of the following oppositions:

INTERNAL versus EXTERNAL

RESTRICTED KNOWLEDGE versus UNRESTRICTED KNOWLEDGE

Internal/External: The example of third person narration given above from *Lord of the Flies* begins by observing characters and events from outside (externally). But third person narration may also provide access to the (internal) consciousness of characters by telling us how they think and feel. Much of D.H. Lawrence's *Lady Chatterley's Lover* (1928), for instance, despite its title, adopts Connie Chatterley's perspective rather than that of her lover, Mellors. The following passage (despite its third person narration) is – with its emphasis on Connie's feelings – fairly representative of the novel as a whole:

Now she came every day to the hens, they were the only things in the world that warmed her heart. Clifford's protestations made her go cold from head to foot. Mrs Bolton's voice made her go cold, and the sound of the business men who came. An occasional letter from Michaelis affected her with the same sense of chill. She felt she would surely die if it lasted much longer.

Yet it was spring, and the bluebells were coming in the wood, and the leaf-buds on the hazels were opening like the spatter of green rain. How terrible it was that it should be spring, and everything cold-hearted, cold-hearted. Only the hens, fluffed so wonderfully on the eggs, were warm with their hot, brooding female bodies! Connie felt herself living on the brink of fainting all the time.

Although this passage, like the rest of the novel, is consistently in the third person, it is nonetheless devoted primarily to the inner sensations of the person it describes. Indeed, rhetorically it is structured around a simple, basic opposition in Connie's sensations between warmth and cold (equivalent to life and death). Significantly, it is difficult to read the penultimate sentence as the narrator's comment. It makes most sense as a piece of free indirect thought belonging in part at least to Connie herself. Third person narration, therefore, has the option of being internal or external, sometimes switching within the same text.

Restricted/Unrestricted: A second distinction may be made in third person narration between narration with no restrictions on the knowable (so-called 'omniscient narration'), and narration with restrictions on the knowable. Indeed, in third person narration we tend to assume that narration is omniscient unless there are indications to the contrary, usually in the foregrounding of a character who – though given to us in the third person – offers a position from which events can be known. Consider the following passage from Henry James's short novel *Daisy Miller* (1879), in which the heroine is observed for us (by a subsidiary character – a young man named

Winterbourne who is sympathetically attracted to Daisy) in conversation with an Italian companion ('her cavalier', or gallant), named Giovanelli:

> Winterbourne stood there: he had turned his eyes towards Daisy and her cavalier. They evidently saw no-one; they were too deeply occupied with each other. When they reached the low garden-wall they stood a moment looking off at the great flat-topped pine-clusters of the Villa Borghese; then Giovanelli seated himself familiarly upon the broad ledge of the wall. The western sun in the opposite sky sent out a brilliant shaft through a couple of cloud bars; whereupon Daisy's companion took her parasol out of her hands and opened it. She came a little nearer and he held the parasol over her; then, still holding it, he let it rest upon her shoulder, so that both their heads were hidden from Winterbourne. This young man lingered a moment, then he began to walk. But he walked – not towards the couple with the parasol; towards the residence of his aunt, Mrs Costello.

In places this passage could be read as simple, omniscient, unrestricted third person. For instance, the following fragment, taken in isolation, seems to be from no one individual's perspective:

> The western sun in the opposite sky sent out a brilliant shaft through a couple of cloud bars; whereupon Daisy's companion took her parasol out of her hands and opened it. She came a little nearer and he held the parasol over her.

However, placed in a larger context this event is clearly framed from Winterbourne's perspective: 'he had *turned his eyes towards* Daisy and her cavalier. They *evidently* saw no-one.' And, later, with the opening of the parasol: 'their heads were hidden from Winterbourne'. Restricting at crucial moments our observation of a central action to what a subsidiary character can see is an important structural device in the novel (as so often in James). Like Winterbourne, we are left at this moment in the narrative in a state of uncertainty concerning the exact nature of Daisy's relationship (sexual or merely flirtatious?) with her cavalier (courtly gentleman or lover?).

Other indications of limited knowledge include phrases of doubt, such as 'it seemed/appeared/looked as if.' The following paragraph, for example, from a story by Nadine Gordimer, uses several signals of doubt (such as 'no doubt', 'somehow' and the question form: 'Hadn't he written a book about the Bay of Pigs?'):

> The voice of the telephone, this time, was American – soft, cautious – no doubt the man thought the line was tapped. Robert Greenman Ceretti, from Washington; while they were talking, she remembered that this was the political columnist who had somehow been connected with the Kennedy administration. Hadn't he written a book about the Bay of Pigs? Anyway, she had certainly seen him quoted.

It is no accident, of course, that this kind of narrowing down of a potentially omniscient narration should come in a narration that aligns itself strongly with the consciousness of one character, even while remaining third person. It is important to recognize, therefore, that third person narration need not always embody objectivity. It can quite easily work from subjective, internal and restricted positions.

3.3 Focalization

We can see, therefore, that the distinction between first person and third person narration is not sufficient in itself to account for different types of point of view. An additional complication arises from the fact that most prose fiction is not stable or homogeneous in the point of view that it adopts, so that it can be quite misleading to describe a story as 'told externally in the third person' (which would imply that

this was a consistent point of view throughout). Even Ernest Hemingway, who might be thought an exemplar of the external third person
viewpoint, does in practice use a variety of modes of narration, often
within the same text, which allow for subjective and internal points
of view. Because of this instability in point of view, some accounts
of narrative (e.g. Bal, 1985; Rimmon-Kenan, 1983; and Simpson,
1993) have refined the account of point of view by developing the
notion of 'focalization'. Focalization refers to the way in which a text
represents the relationship between who 'experiences' and what is
experienced. The one who experiences is termed the 'focalizer', and
who or what the focalizer experiences is then called the 'focalized'.
Focalization falls into two main types: external focalization, where
an anonymous, unidentified voice situated outside the text functions
as focalizer; and character focalization, where phenomena are presented as experienced by a character within the story.

It is possible then to map shifts and tendencies in focalization
within any one text by using the following simple notation:

F'r = Focalizer
E   = External
C   = Character
1   = First person
3   = Third person
F'd = Focalized phenomenon

Thus:

External focalizer   = EF'r
Character focalizer (first person)   = CF'r1
Character focalizer (third person) = CF'r3
Focalized phenomenon   = F'd

Take the following idealized examples of differing focalization
from three hypothetical narrations:

(1) Despite closing the windows, I could hear noises from the
     beach all that sleepless night.

(2) Even with the windows closed, she could not shut out the noises from the beach.

(3) Even with the windows closed, the noises from the beach were audible all night.

In each example, 'noises from the beach' are the focalized phenomenon, hence [F'd]. In (1) 'I' is the focalizer, hence [CF'r1]. In (2) 'she' is the focalizer, hence [CF'r3]. In (3) no-one is identified as the focalizer and the noise is reported by an unidentified narrator from a position potentially outside the constructed world of the fiction, hence [EF'r]. Thus, the focalization structure of the three examples may be rendered in notational terms as follows:

(1)   CF'r1('I') $\rightarrow$ F'd ('noises from the beach')
(2)   CF'r3('she') $\rightarrow$ F'd ('the noises from the beach')
(3)   EF'r $\rightarrow$ F'd ('the noises from the beach')

These examples, as if from separate narrations, have been constructed to display differences of focalization. In practice, focalization within a narrative text tends to shift from sentence to sentence and sometimes can alter even within the same sentence. In the later history of the novel it is hardly ever stable and consistent throughout a text. The advantage of the notation lies in the way it can be applied to display these focalization shifts in terms of who is experiencing what and how from sentence to sentence.

Crucial evidence for deciding who is focalizing is the presence or absence of verbs of experiencing such as 'look', 'see', 'touch', 'smell', etc. Consider the following example from Rosamund Lehmann's *The Weather in the Streets* (1936) (the sentences have been numbered):

(1) She [Olivia] ran down to the next floor, telephoned for a taxi, then opened the door of Etty's bedroom, adjoining the sitting room. (2) Silence and obscurity greeted her; and a smell compounded of powder, scent, toilet creams and chocolate truffles.

In the first sentence Olivia and her actions are focalized from without by an unidentified focalizer. In the second sentence, however, the smell and the silence are impressions that belong to Olivia rather than to the external focalizer of the first sentence. The focalization shifts therefore from external focalization (EF'r) to character focalization (CF'r). This can be summed up as follows:

Sentence 1: EF'r (unspecified)   →   F'd (Olivia)
Sentence 2: CF'r3 (Olivia/She)   →   F'd (silence, smell, etc.)

Similar shifts can be detected in the following passage from the same book:

(3) Between stages of dressing and washing she [Olivia] packed a hasty suitcase. (4) Pack the red dress, wear the dark brown tweed, Kate's cast off, well-cut, with my nice jumper, lime green, becoming, pack the other old brown jumper – That's about all.

Again, the extract begins as externally focalized, but in the second sentence there is a switch to Olivia's 'inner speech' or thoughts, as she does her packing (presented in 'free indirect style'). Moving into the character's consciousness in this way entails a change of focalization from external focalization to character focalization. Here again, we can summarize:

Sentence 3: EF'r (unspecified)   →   F'd (Olivia packing)
Sentence 4: CF'r1 (Olivia/my)   →   F'd (Olivia packing)

On this occasion, the notation helps to highlight, not just a shift in focalization, but the way in which Olivia in this passage comes to be the focalizer of her own actions. For a moment she is the object of her own subjective consciousness in a way that is both intimate and distanced. In ways such as these, the concept of focalization can become an important supplement to notions of point of view because it prompts close attention to the shifts, developments, and balances within point of view within a particular text. *The Weather in the Streets*, for instance, moves between external focalization and character focalization that is centred primarily on Olivia, who figures sometimes as third person, sometimes as first person. These subtle variations help construct her as at once somehow both subject and object of the narrative.

Focalization can in this way be studied in terms of how it is realized from one sentence to another in a text. It may be observed at the level of the form of the text. But focalization at a deeper level is more than this. Patterns of focalization are at once the expression and construction of types of both consciousness and self-consciousness. In that respect, *The Weather in the Streets* is very much a novel of the first half of the twentieth century. It is quite distinct, for instance, from *Robinson Crusoe*, even though Crusoe also figures as both subject and object of his own narrative. The relentless 'I' of Crusoe's narrative seems to present the human subject as individual, stable, unified and separate. The shifting patterns of focalization in *The Weather in the Streets* on the other hand seem to present an idea of subjectivity as split and dispersed at the very moment that it becomes possible to grasp it in a self-conscious way.

ACTIVITY 3.1

The following text is the complete version of a story by Ernest Hemingway. It is narrated in the third person and involves two main protagonists, a man and a woman.

A Very Short Story

One hot evening in Padua they carried him up on to the roof and he could look out over the top of the town. There were chimney swifts in the sky. After a while it got dark and the searchlights came out. The others went down and took the bottles with them. He and Luz could hear them below on the   5
balcony. Luz sat on the bed. She was cool and fresh in the hot night.

Luz stayed on night duty for three months. They were glad
to let her. When they operated on him she prepared him for
the operating table; and they had a joke about friend or enema. 10
He went under the anaesthetic holding tight on to himself
so he would not blab about anything during the silly, talky
time. After he got on crutches he used to take the temperatures
so Luz would not have to get up from the bed. There were
only a few patients, and they all knew about it. They all liked 15
Luz. As he walked back along the halls he thought of Luz in
his bed.

Before he went back to the front they went into the Duomo
and prayed. It was dim and quiet, and there were other people
praying. They wanted to get married, but there was not enough 20
time for the banns, and neither of them had birth certificates.
They felt as though they were married, but they wanted
everyone to know about it, and to make it so they could not
lose it.

Luz wrote him many letters that he never got until after 25
the armistice. Fifteen came in a bunch to the front and he
sorted them by the dates and read them all straight through.
They were all about the hospital, and how much she loved
him and how it was impossible to get along without him and
how terrible it was missing him at night. 30

After the armistice they agreed he should go home to get a
job so they might be married. Luz would not come home until
he had a good job and could come to New York to meet her.
It was understood he would not drink, and he did not want to
see his friend or anyone in the States. Only to get a job and be 35
married. On the train from Padua to Milan they quarrelled
about her not being willing to come home at once. When
they had to say good-bye, in the station at Milan, they kissed
good-bye, but were not finished with the quarrel. He felt sick
about saying good-bye like that. 40

He went to America on a boat from Genoa. Luz went
back to Pordenone to open a hospital. It was lonely and rainy

there, and there was a battalion of arditi quartered in the
town. Living in the muddy, rainy town in the winter, the
major of the battalion made love to Luz, and she had never   45
known Italians before, and finally wrote to the States that
theirs had been only a boy and girl affair. She was sorry,
and she knew he would probably not be able to understand,
but might some day forgive her, and be grateful to her, and
she expected, absolutely unexpectedly, to be married in the   50
spring. She loved him as always, but she realized now it was
only a boy and girl love. She hoped he would have a great career,
and believed in him absolutely. She knew it was for the best.

    The major did not marry her in the spring, or any other
time. Luz never got an answer to the letter to Chicago about   55
it. A short time after he contracted gonorrhea from a sales
girl in a Loop department store while riding in a taxicab
through Lincoln Park.

1 Read through the story and then try altering the mode of
    narration by transposing the text into first person narration
    from the woman's point of view. (Thus, 'Luz sat on the bed'
    becomes transposed to 'I sat on the bed'.)

2 Write down any peculiar or incongruous sentences that re-
    sult from this transposition and try and detail the grounds
    on which they are peculiar.

3 Now transpose the text into first person narration from the
    man's point of view. (Thus, 'they carried him up on to the roof'
    becomes transposed to 'they carried me up on to the roof'.)

4 Note again any peculiarities or incongruities that result.

5 Which transposition of point of view has worked best and
    why? What does it suggest about the original, third person
    mode of narration? Did it involve an implicit bias; and, if so,
    in favour of whom? What other textual mechanisms might
    support this bias?

Reading

Bal, Mieke (1985) *Narratology: Introduction to the Theory of Narrative*, Toronto: Toronto University Press.

Branigan, E. (1984) *Point of View in the Cinema*, New York: Mouton.

Fowler, R. (1986) *Linguistic Criticism*, Oxford: Oxford University Press, Chapter 9, pp. 127–46.

Furniss, T.E. and Bath, M. (1996) *Reading Poetry: An Introduction*, London: Longman, Chapter 7.

Rimmon-Kenan, S. (1983) *Narrative Fiction: Contemporary Poetics*, London: Methuen, Chapter 6, pp. 71–85.

Scholes, R. (1982) *Semiotics and Interpretation*, New Haven, CT: Yale University Press.

Simpson, P. (1993) *Language, Ideology and Point of View*, London: Routledge.

Uspensky, B. (1973) *A Poetics of Composition*, Berkeley, CA: University of California Press.

SECTION
THREE

LEADING QUESTIONS

1

Seeing Through Language

We all encounter literature in a variety of ways. Our parents read us bedtime stories. We progress to comics, to stories, to whole novels. Perhaps you acquire a taste for science fiction or bodice-ripping romances. Your teachers may get you to read novels or poems as background to history or sociology. Or possibly you discover how pleasant it is to escape from tedious reality into the 'world' of a book.

It can be argued that studying Literature at A-level differs from these normal encounters with literature in two ways. The first is that the books you study are not determined by your own taste but by the Examiners and what they consider Good. The second is that you are asked not only to read critically but to write critically too. You will be expected to discuss not only *what* a writer writes, but also *how* that writer writes. In other words, you are being asked to try your hand at literary criticism. As you are probably aware, there are different kinds of literary criticism (which have different sets of rules). There is, for example, the kind of essay you will have to write on your set texts ('Is Hamlet really mad?' and that sort of thing). There are learned books on the works of one particular author. There are those daunting books with titles something like *Concepts of Nature in Eighteenth-Century English Verse.* And then there's the kind of criticism this book is mostly about: the kind that, for convenience, we will call by its traditional name, Practical Criticism. This is the kind of criticism you'll need some skill in when you are asked to write about particular poems or particular pieces of prose.

What is Practical Criticism?

'Practical Criticism' has a no-nonsense, sleeves-rolled-up, hands-on sort of a sound to it; and that's appropriate enough, in a way, because it involves the close, careful scrutiny of individual poems and prose extracts. It's a way of getting to the meanings of a piece of writing by looking at the way it's put together. It's a technique that grew from a book called *Practical Criticism* by a scholar called I. A. Richards, published in 1929. You will not be surprised to learn that the technique has been rethought and revised a good deal since then. Let's begin by summarizing the basic principles of Practical Criticism as evolved by Richards and other critics associated with him. Very briefly, they are these:

1 The text (of a poem, especially) is self-contained and self-defining. It is what it is, and it contains its meanings within itself.

2 The text is what we might call 'organic'. That is to say, its various elements (the meanings of individual words, their sounds, their rhythms when grouped together, and so on) relate to and depend on each other. As critical readers, we should be trying to understand the 'internal dynamics' of the piece and the way these various elements work together.

3 The way to an understanding, an appreciation, of a work of literature is through a close reading, or scrutiny, of its language.

These principles are a bit hard to grasp at first, but never mind. The ideas that lie behind them, though, are rather important, and you should give them some thought. In the same order, they are:

1 The historical, social and political influences upon a work of literature are largely irrelevant. So are the details of the writer's life. Accordingly, if we are reading a poem by Shakespeare, it doesn't matter a hoot when and where he

was when he wrote it, or what his political views were, or who he was married to. In fact, it wouldn't make any difference – to the poem – if 'Shakespeare' was someone else altogether. What matters is what is there, in the poem.

2 A good reader is an analytical reader. If a reader is to appreciate how the different elements of a piece of writing interact (and this applies especially to poetry) then that reader has to be able to separate these elements out. Equally importantly, that reader must be able to put them back together again, because that's how you arrive at a 'reading' of the poem as a whole.

3 Whatever else a written work may be, it is primarily a linguistic structure. It is an organisation of words.

Principle number 1 and Idea number 1 are no longer widely accepted, and there's no need for you to accept them either. What they suggest, after all, is that something called 'literature' exists independently of the people who create it. They suggest that the personality of the writer, and the society in which that writer lives or lived, are unimportant when we read and think about what he or she wrote. The implication is that literature exists at some sort of 'pure' level, detached from history, politics, sex, money and all the other messy things that surround any writer's life. Theoretically, according to this view of literature, it is largely irrelevant whether the writer of a poem or novel is a man or a woman. This is not a view that is taken very seriously nowadays. It is fairly obvious that, for all its uniqueness, any literary work must be related in some way to its social and historical context; and this means that this context must be relevant to its meaning. It is also fairly obvious that any poem or novel or whatever is, in a loose sense, autobiographical, because writers write from their own experience and view of the world. This means that the events and circumstances of the writer's life may well be important when it comes to trying to understand his or her work. However, the idea of the 'self-contained text' is useful in one respect: it warns us against the temptation of trying to 'explain' a writer's work in simple biographical terms. In other words, while it is, of course, likely that a writer's life-experiences influence the way that person writes, we shouldn't assume that these experiences are a 'key' to anything. It would be silly to think that a poem about loneliness, let's say, can be easily understood if we know that the poet's mother ran off with a soldier when the poet was nine years old. In practice this means that if you do dig into a writer's life and times, and you come up with something you think illuminates one of that writer's poems, you will be expected to argue your case quite carefully.

We're left with the remaining two principles of Practical Criticism and their implications. These are more important to you because they still apply; examiners will expect you to understand and respect these ideas, especially when you are writing about individual poems or pieces of prose. We'll take them one at a time.

To say that a poem is 'organic' is to say that it resembles an organism (a living thing) more than it resembles a machine. You can take the fan belt off a car engine and what you have left is still recognisably a car engine. If you chop out a line or a stanza of a poem (or abridge or censor a novel) you change it radically. This is because poems (especially, but it's true of prose works as well) are highly *integrated*; their component parts are interdependent. To give a very crude example, you could replace a word in a line of poetry with another word or phrase which means much the same thing, and the sense of that line would remain the same. But the effect on another element of the poem might be quite drastic. If instead of

The curfew tolls the knell of parting day

you wrote

The curfew tolls the knell at the end of the day

you wouldn't change the meaning but you would destroy the *rhythm* of the line.

Practical Criticism demands that you be abnormally aware of the way that these different elements of a piece of writing interrelate. It requires a close attention to detail. You have to accept from the outset that it is a specialised sort of a task which requires specialist skills.

Now for the third of these Principles and Ideas: that understanding a piece of writing depends upon a close and careful scrutiny of its language, because all literary works are, first and foremost, words on a page. This may seem ridiculously obvious, yet many students are reluctant to accept it. One reason for this (and here you have to imagine the authors of this book smugly stroking their long grey beards) is that students are still young enough to be in a hurry. They – you – are impatient to get 'through' the language in order to get at 'Meanings', to get at 'Ideas', 'Interpretations', 'Insights into Life' and whatever. (This is the 'message-hunting' approach to literature.) The destination, they feel, is more important than the journey. It isn't. There may not be a destination. Another reason is that grappling with language is hard work; strangely enough, it is much easier to ramble on about the philosophical or political implications of a poem than it is to struggle to see how the poet put the thing together. Another problem is that we can only describe what language does by using language. This means that in order to discuss how someone else uses language, you have to develop a pretty sophisticated language of your own – and that too is hard work.

Is there such a thing as 'literary language'?

There was a time when there was such a thing as 'poetic language'. It was full of musical sound-effects, the lines always rhymed, it was heavily figurative (it contained lots of metaphors and similes), there would be capital letters at the beginning of every line (and liberally scattered about elsewhere, too), and its subject would be some noble or tragic feeling. Something like this, in fact:

It was a dismal and fearful night:
Scarce could the Morn drive on th'unwilling Light,
When Sleep, Death's image, left my troubled breast
By something liker Death possest.

We can no longer expect literary language to announce itself so loudly or signal to us so energetically. Certainly in much modern writing the distinction between 'literary' and 'ordinary' language is very blurred. We think it would be best to abandon the idea of a special literary language, a language peculiar to imaginative writing. It will be much more useful for you to have a few flexible techniques for getting at what writers do with language. Here are four ideas for you to consider:

1 In literature, language tends to draw attention to itself:

Even on Central Avenue, not the quietest-dressed street in the world, he looked about as inconspicuous as a tarantula on a slice of angel food.

Raymond Chandler: Farewell My Lovely

In other words, he was loudly dressed. In the novel from which this is taken, it is preceded by ninety words describing this character's outfit, so we know that already. But the phrase 'as a tarantula on a slice of angel food' isn't there to convey information. It jumps off the page at you. (Critics sometimes use the word 'foregrounding' to describe this technique.) It shocks, and it grabs your attention (which may have been wandering). Like the man's clothes, it is 'loud': the extremely different associations of 'tarantula' and 'angel' collide with a bang. And perhaps you stop for a moment while across your mind scuttles the thought of what it would be like to be served a dessert with a huge hairy spider sitting on it. The phrase also contains suggestions about this character which might become relevant as the story progresses: poisonous, dangerous, out of place.

2 **Language is sometimes transparent, sometimes opaque.**

A **Slice an onion and fry it in a little oil until lightly browned.**

B **An odour of frying wafts at the opening of the page, of onion in fact, of onion being fried, a bit scorched, because in the onion there are veins that turn violet and then brown, and especially the edge, the margin, of each little sliver of onion becomes black before golden, it is the juice of the onion that is carbonised, passing through a series of olfactory and chromatic nuances, all enveloped in the smell of simmering oil.**

Italo Calvino: If On A Winter's Night A Traveller . . .

The purpose of transparent language is to convey information or instruction. Reading sentence A in a cookery book, there would be no point dwelling on its language. You look 'through' the language, so to speak, at the things – onion and oil – and what you are supposed to do with them. In that sort of situation, language that drew attention to itself would simply get in the way, would hold you up, and dinner would never get cooked.

While still on the subject of onions, sentence B could hardly be more different. Here it is the language itself which is noticeable. We look (at first, anyway) *at* it rather than through it; it is much more opaque. The language in this sentence draws attention to itself by being so very busy. We'll not go on at length about it, but you should perhaps notice a few things. First of all, there is the way the sentence moves, the way it hurries along from comma to comma not quite able to stop. Then there is the insistent repetition of the word 'onion', and the way the writer seems so eager to make everything very precise. If one word doesn't do the job well enough, he helps it along with another: 'onion being fried, a bit scorched' and 'the edge, the margin'. There are strong contrasts in the 'feel' of different words and phrases: compare the bluntness of 'a bit scorched' with the elaborate phrase 'a series of olfactory and chromatic nuances' (which means 'shades of smell and colour'). This sentence is playing a game, sharing a joke with the reader: this description of onions being fried is, the writer pretends, so concrete and realistic that smell actually 'wafts' off the page. (And the fact that it doesn't, really, is his way of pointing out that words on a page remain only words on a page no matter how hard we work them.)

3 The meaning of words depends on and changes with the words' context.

At a simple level, this is obvious. Many English words are capable of a number of different meanings. It is only in conjunction with other words that they achieve a particular meaning:

	bar
colour	bar
	bar one
gold	bar
	bar sinister
wine	bar

You can probably think of hundreds more examples. You might like to see how many variations you can make on the meanings of *post, fire, house, water.*

Here is an example of how meaning can be modulated by context in a more subtle way. The following short extract describes how the first warnings of the Indian Mutiny reach an outpost of the British Empire.

> **The first sign of trouble at Krishnapur came with a mysterious distribution of chapatis, made of coarse flour and about the size and thickness of a biscuit; towards the end of February 1857 they swept the countryside like an epidemic . . .**
>
> **The Collector was busy at that time. In addition to his official duties, which had become swollen and complicated by the illness of the Joint Magistrate, he had a number of domestic matters on his mind; his wife, too, had been in poor health for the past few months and must now be sent home before the hot weather.**
>
> *J. G. Farrell: The Siege of Krishnapur*

The words 'swollen and complicated' can be taken at face value as meaning that the Collector's work-load had increased and become more difficult. ('Collector, here means Chief Administrator, by the way.) But the phrase occurs in a passage which also contains the words 'epidemic', 'illness' and 'poor health', and it takes on an extra shade of meaning. To overstate it a little, there's the suggestion that the Collector's duties have been infected by disease. In this way, the phrase contributes to the picture being built up of a colonial society that is 'sick' – perhaps in more ways than one.

4 Language can be used as a code.

A code is 'a language familiar to both writer and reader (or speaker and listener)'. This does not mean simply English or Arabic, say, as those languages would be understood by the people that happen to speak them. It also means the way that language is used by members of the same group, or class, or profession, for example, when addressing each other. Codes of this sort imply shared interests, experiences or values. Judges and barristers have a language code (which the rest of us are not meant to understand). So do Rastafarians. And Freemasons. It is possible that your family uses a code which outsiders would not fully understand. The language code of *The Sun* is obviously different from the language code of *The Guardian.* As an A-Level student, you will be expected to understand the language code of teachers and examiners (and the authors of textbooks).

In literature, certain words or phrases or grammatical forms may contain meanings that are different from, or more than, their literal meanings. They can conjure up ideas or associations in the minds of readers who 'know what they mean'. With this in mind, look at the following four sentences, and before we say anything about them, spend a minute or two thinking about what they convey to you:

A She had blue eyes and blonde hair.
B She was a blue-eyed blonde.

C Blue-eyed, blonde-haired Michelle Williams, 24, told the Court that on the night in question she had stayed at home doing the *Times* crossword.

D Azure were her eyes, golden her hair.

Sentence A is seemingly 'transparent'. It appears to refer neutrally to objective facts about a person's appearance. But it also operates as a code, because blue eyes and blonde hair is one of the clichés, or stereotypes, of female attractiveness. It is an image, or 'trigger', that men are conditioned to respond to. The sentence is thus capable of the hidden meaning 'she was sexually attractive'. In this particular sentence, however, the 'coded message' is optional, because the way that the sentence is constructed does not exclude the possibility that she had other things as well – a degree in Political Science, or a wet nappy, or whatever. In other words, she is not completely trapped within the sentence.

Now try these questions:

1 **The structure of sentence B is only slightly different to that of sentence A. What effect does this slight change have on the code that it carries?**

2 **Where would you expect to find sentence C? How do you respond to the statement it makes? Do you take this sentence to be 'neutral' or 'objective' reportage? Do you think that its writer intended you to take it as neutral, objective reportage?**

On the face of it, sentence D does not seem to belong with the others. Simply 'translated', it means the same as sentence A, but you probably recognised straight away that it is meant to be 'poetic'. It clearly signals its poetic intentions with certain linguistic devices, which are inverted syntax ('were her eyes' instead of 'her eyes were'); the omission of 'was' between 'golden' and 'her'; the use of the more melodious 'azure' rather than plain 'blue'; putting a sort of rhythm into the line (two emphases, or 'beats' before the comma, on 'azure' and 'eyes', and two after the comma, on 'gold' and 'hair'). Also, 'azure' is a much more opaque or attention-seeking word than 'blue'. As well as being another name for the colour, it is also another name for the precious stone lapis lazuli; it also means, the dictionary tells us, 'the clear blue of the unclouded sky' and 'the unclouded vault of heaven'. The associations of gold are obvious. Clearly, then, the writer of sentence D is manipulating language a great deal. You could say that he is 'interfering' with the 'plain' language of sentence A. Why is he? Well, what this writer is trying to do – rather desperately – is block or 'intercept' the coded messages we get from sentences A and B. He doesn't want the vulgar interpretation 'she was sexually attractive' put on his words. Instead, he is trying to convey a message something like 'she was rare, heavenly, a treasure'. Unfortunately for him, however, he has merely replaced a sexual cliché with a poetic one; he has tried to refresh a tired old descriptive cliché – and failed.

Now let's try applying those four ideas – language drawing attention to itself, transparency/opacity, meaning changing with context, and code – to a poem.

You may remember those simple Reading Scheme books for very young children. They starred a rosy-cheeked middle-class brother and sister called Janet and John (or Peter and Jane). They had a large yellow dog of some sort. The language of these books was, naturally, elementary and repetitious: 'Here is Janet. Here is John. Here is the dog', and so on. A language so 'plain' and 'transparent' it seems completely devoid of poetic possibilities. Here is what Wendy Cope does with it:

Reading Scheme
>Here is Peter. Here is Jane. They like fun.
>Jane has a big doll. Peter has a ball.
>Look, Jane, look! Look at the dog! See him run!
>
>Here is Mummy. She has baked a bun.
>Here is the milkman. He has come to call.
>Here is Peter. Here is Jane. They like fun.

Go Peter! Go Jane! Come, milkman come!
The milkman likes Mummy. She likes them all.
Look, Jane, look! Look at the dog! See him run!

Here are the curtains. They shut out the sun.
Let us peep! On tiptoe Jane! You are small!
Here is Peter. Here is Jane. They like fun.

I hear a car Jane. The milkman looks glum.
Here is Daddy in his car. Daddy is tall.
Look, Jane, look! Look at the dog! See him run!

Daddy looks very cross. Has he a gun?
Up milkman! Up milkman! Over the wall!
Here is Peter. Here is Jane. They like fun.
Look, Jane, look! Look at the dog! See him run!

Wendy Cope

It's fairly obvious that Wendy Cope is making comedy here by shuffling together two very incongruous clichés: the easy-to-read style of the children's book and the corny old joke about Mummy doing Something Naughty with the milkman and being caught at it by Daddy. Try answering the following questions about the poem:

1 What is your first reaction to the opening lines, finding them in an adult poem in this book rather than in an 'Early Reader'?
2 What do you notice about the rhymes in the poem?
3 What do you notice about the use of repetition?
4 At what point in the poem do you begin to suspect that something odd is going on?
5 Who speaks line 7?
6 Who might 'them all' in line 8 refer to?
7 Does the word 'fun' have the same meaning at the end of the poem as it did at the beginning?

Here are the answers. (If you haven't tried working them out for yourself yet, don't read them!)

1 Quite simply, you ought to be surprised. You ought to do a 'double-take'.

2 There are only two: words that rhyme with 'fun' and those that rhyme with 'ball'.

3 There's a lot of it, and it is arranged in a formal pattern. The lines that begin with 'Here is Peter' and 'Look, Jane' alternately end each 'verse' and form a final couplet.

4 At lines 7 and 8.

5 Mummy. She's telling Peter and Jane to get lost, and inviting the milkman in.

6 'Them all' might mean Peter, Jane, the dog and the milkman; or all milkmen; or all the men who come calling (if you've got a suspicious mind).

7 No. At the end of the poem; 'fun' has come to include what Mummy does with the milkman, and also the spectacle of seeing Daddy, armed with a gun, chasing an adulterous milkman over the garden wall. Not the same thing at all.

Now let's try and make some connections between these answers and the ideas about language that we put to you earlier.

One way that language – or anything else, for that matter – can draw attention to itself is by being out of context (like that tarantula). In its 'proper place' – in a Reading Scheme book – the sentence 'Here is Peter' carries very little meaning. Its only function is to point to a picture of Peter. As language, it is 'transparent'. But when this sentence appears in a collection of poems for grown-ups (and without a picture of Peter) we do not simply look through it. We look at it. We suspect that it has something other than its normal significance.

The first lines of this poem operate as a kind of code. The primitive sentences 'Here is Peter. Here is Jane. They like fun' conjure up, or evoke, the world depicted in those early Reading Scheme books. It is a world in which healthy, improbably well-behaved, fair-haired children frolic about with their bouncy golden retriever in a sunlit, peaceful suburban garden while Mummy is in the kitchen and Daddy is at the office. A world, in short, of security, respectability, niceness, and – above all – innocence. (Needless to say, if you never read those books as a child you won't 'get' all this. But then, as we said earlier, that is characteristic of codes; you have to be a member of a group 'in the know' to get the message.)

The simple rhyme-scheme and the insistent repetition mimic the language of the Reading Scheme book. Before long, we realise that this is a **parody**. This should 'click' with you when you begin to think that Mummy's relationship with the milkman is not quite what it should be.

In the context of the poem, the meaning of the innocent word 'fun' is undermined. It becomes much more ambiguous and loses its association with 'harmless'.

If we add all this up, we can get to a 'reading' of the poem. What Wendy Cope does is set up the idealised, fanciful world of the Reading Scheme books and then subvert it by introducing the sordid adult activities of infidelity, jealousy and violence. She does this, presumably, because she believes that world and its 'innocence' to be phoney, dishonest. This may be taking a jokey poem too seriously for your taste. Perhaps it is. One last observation, then: this poem is a story of sexual misbehaviour told in the simple, naïve language of children. The language is inappropriate to its subject. Put another way, there is a deliberate discrepancy, or conflict, between subject and language. This is a form of irony – but we'll come to that later. In the meantime, try writing just a few sentences on the strange things writers are doing with language in each of these brief extracts:

A Compare 'She was not very upset by the death of her husband'
   with   'Her hair has turned quite gold with grief'.

B Tell me, O Octopus, I begs,
   Is those things arms, or is they legs?
   I marvel at thee, Octopus;
   If I were thou, I'd call me Us.

Ogden Nash: The Octopus

C When as in silks my Julia goes,
   Then, then (methinks) how sweetly flows
   That liquifaction of her clothes.

Robert Herrick: Upon Julia's Clothes

D He snorted and hit me in the solar plexus.
   I bent over and took hold of the room with both hands
   and spun it. When I had it nicely spinning I gave it a full
   swing and hit myself on the back of my head with the floor.
   This made me lose my balance temporarily and while I
   was thinking about how to regain it a wet towel began to
   slap at my face and I opened my eyes. The face of Henry
   Eichelberger was close to mine and bore a certain appearance
   of solicitude.

Raymond Chandler: Pearls Are A Nuisance

E One humid afternoon a visitor did arrive to disturb Rottcodd
   as he lay deeply hammocked, for his siesta was broken sharply
   by a rattling of the door handle which was apparently performed in lieu of the more popular practice of knocking at
   the panels. The sound echoed down the long room and then
   settled into the fine dust on the boarded floor. The sunlight
   squeezed itself between the thin cracks of the window blind.

Mervyn Peake: Titus Groan

2

Metaphor 1: Holy Kitchens and Drunken Pilots

This chapter introduces the subject of metaphor. We're going to be a bit technical, a bit analytical, and even a bit historical. The danger is that we might lose sight of the fact that metaphor is a very basic yet magical linguistic device. So before we start looking into what metaphor is and how it works, we should look at some of the things it can do.

This chapter is, for the most part, a selection of pieces of writing which (with one exception) use metaphor in ways which we hope you'll find entertaining and interesting. For the time being, let's define metaphor as a figure of speech which brings together two different things and creates some kind of similarity between them. It is quite normal, for example, to compare an angry person to a kettle: 'he was boiling with rage'.

Metaphor is often the only way we can think and speak about abstract things which we cannot experience with our physical senses. Take, for instance, the familiar concept 'school', or 'college'. Is 'school' the building itself, or the teachers, or the teachers and the students? Is it the relentless daily process of transferring knowledge, or is it the name you give to the sum total of all those moments of pain and boredom and discovery and success? Metaphor can be a short cut through the complication of saying what such an abstract concept means to you. Have a look at this list of choices:

school or college is
  a prison

a giant anthill

a grey filing cabinet with many drawers

a hurdle race

a large family with its own rules and language

Which of these comparisons seems to you the most appropriate? Why does it? (And if they are all way off beam, what is your suggestion?) If you did find one of these comparisons valid, then obviously you detected similarities between it and school. At the same time, though, you will have 'filtered out' some of the obvious differences between the two things. We can all recognise what the similarities are between an anthill and a busy school, but when we see that comparison we filter out a great deal of what we know about ants; in other words, we don't actually see students as having six legs and antennae. What we mean is that students at school are like ants in that they . . .

Here's another list to choose from:

knowledge is

a vast, mysterious and dusty library with mazes of shelves, staffed and guarded by uniformed attendants

a totally bald, swollen human head covered in strange bumps and ridges

a huge and forbidding tree with innumerable branches, and each of its millions and millions of leaves is printed with a single word

a large container of coloured liquid, from which emerge numerous coloured tubes, all labelled differently, each with a tap at the end

a darkened room in which sits a small TV monitor chattering away to itself and filling its screen with colourful charts and diagrams

Again, which of those analogies made the most sense to you, or had the most impact on you, and why? (And again, can you do better?)

Here's another:

childhood is
   a large open field in the mountains full of flowers and butterflies
   a small room in which there is a loudspeaker softly issuing orders
     which make only partial sense
   a doll's house in which every single article is labelled with a name
     written in lower case letters
   a cardboard box containing old clothes, a few broken toys and
     some dog-eared reading books

Most of you are less distant from your childhood than the writers of this book are. Your relative closeness to it will no doubt affect the way you choose metaphors to describe it. Invent two metaphors of your own which convey your feelings about childhood more accurately and effectively than ours do.

Now that you have done a bit of preliminary metaphorical thinking, let's go on to look at a few short passages of prose. Generally it is true that prose is less densely metaphorical than poetry, because prose usually needs to have 'transparent' passages which give the reader information about things and actions and so forth. In prose, therefore, metaphors tend to be more isolated and distinct, which makes them a little easier to pick out and analyse. Still, we don't want to get bogged down in huge and mapless categories like 'prose' and 'poetry' just yet. Here's a brief extract from a short story about life 'below stairs':

And, indeed, is there not something holy about a great kitchen? Those vaults of soot-darkened stone far above me, where the hams and strings of onions and bunches of dried herbs dangle, looking somewhat like the regimental banners that unfurl above the aisles of old churches. The cool, echoing flags scrubbed spotless twice a day by votive persons on their knees. The scoured gleam of row upon row of metal vessels dangling from hooks or reposing on their shelves till needed with the air

of so many chalices waiting for the sacrament of food. And the range like an altar, yes, an altar, before which my mother bowed in perpetual homage, a fringe of sweat upon her upper lip and fire glowing in her cheeks.

Angela Carter: The Kitchen Child

1 What signs are there in the passage that Angela Carter wants to get her metaphor across forcefully and suggest that she isn't in dead earnest about it?

2 The very fact that a kitchen is not, really, very much like a church is what makes the metaphor surprising and amusing. Yet metaphor is meant, supposedly, to compare things that are somehow similar. Why is the difference between a kitchen and a church important to the effect that Angela Carter is trying to produce?

The extract from *The Kitchen Child* establishes a metaphor (kitchen as church) and then goes on to elaborate it in different ways. For obvious reasons, this technique is known as **extended metaphor.**

The next piece is from F. Scott Fitzgerald's *The Great Gatsby.* The narrator of the novel, Nick Carraway, is describing his encounter with two young and rich women:

We walked through a high hallway into a bright rosy-coloured space, fragilely bound into the house by french windows at either end. The windows were ajar and gleaming white against the fresh grass outside that seemed to grow a little way into the house. A breeze blew through the room, blew curtains in at one end and out at the other like pale flags, twisting them up toward the frosted wedding cake of the ceiling, and then rippled over the wine-coloured rug, making a shadow on it as the wind does on the sea.

The only completely stationary object in the room was an enormous couch on which two young women were buoyed up as though upon an anchored balloon. They were both in white, and their dresses were rippling and fluttering as if they had just been blown back in after a short trip around the house. I must have stood for a few moments listening to the whip and snap of the curtains and the groan of a picture on the wall. Then there was a boom as Tom Buchanan shut the rear windows and the caught wind died out about the room, and the curtains and the rugs and the two young women ballooned slowly to the floor.

F. Scott Fitzgerald: The Great Gatsby

1 What do you consider to be the 'key' words in that first paragraph, and what do they tell you about Carraway's impressions of the house?

2 The second paragraph contains a 'hidden' metaphor. The two women look as if they had been 'blown back' after a 'short flight'. What are they being compared to? How might this underlying metaphor affect our attitudes towards these two characters? Why might Fitzgerald want to keep this metaphor understated (as compared to, say, the very foregrounded metaphors in the passage by Dickens)?

3

The Angel and the Private Eye

Once upon a time . . .

This chapter is about the ways writers of fiction use different narrative techniques in order to produce different effects upon you when you're reading, in order to persuade you to interpret and understand what you are reading in different ways. The subject of 'narrative method' should be of interest to any would-be novelist or critic because it involves the actual working practices of individual writers and the sorts of decisions that they have to make before they tell a story. Just as poems are made of formal patterns as well as being kinds of information, so narratives are formal arrangements of their material.

'Telling stories' involves a whole series of decisions and choices, some of which may be your own, some of which may be forced upon you by the kind of story you are telling, the attitude you have towards your material, the sort of relationship that you desire to establish with your readers (or listeners), and the different reactions you want from them.

Unusual for a Monday

Let's imagine that we want to tell a story about an unexpected visitor to a classroom. There are probably hundreds of different ways in which this event can be told, but here are six 'standard' narrative approaches. We'll begin with the 'buttonholing-the-reader-in-order-to-get-a-hearing' approach and go on from there:

1   What do you know, dear reader, of angels: those pretty but sexless beings adorned with golden tresses of hair and feathered wings that peep over the shoulder and drag at heel? They live in Victorian engravings and Mediaeval Bibles, but no one seems to see them very often in our drab and unimaginative century. You must believe in them though, because, if you do not, then this story will remain as words on the page and become neither pictures in your mind nor feelings in your heart.

2   Mr Peet stood at the front of the class and opened his own dull brown copy of a school edition of Chaucer's *The Merchant's Tale*. His students, with considerable reluctance, found their dull brown books. Outside, the wind was blowing furiously against the side of the nissen hut classroom and slamming rain against the rusty metal windows and the corrugated asbestos roof. Not so far away, at the eastern edge of the Atlantic Ocean, huge, grey and magnificent waves were rolling towards the Cornish coast and keeping fishermen indoors. The lesson dragged on '"To doon hir ful plesance . . . " Now, who can translate that for us all? Higgens?' The students all giggled; they knew this quote was probably rude, and that Higgens never did his homework, and so didn't know what they all knew: that this was one of Chaucer's 'earthy' bits, and so good for a laugh. Then Peet noticed something in the corner of the room. Nothing precise at first, just a sort of gilt presence. There was something over there that had been transparent and was slowly becoming opaque, standing quietly by the wall near the classroom door. It was a kind of golden cloud, an outline of something, as yet undefined. Could it be that he was, at last, going mad?

3   There's something weird happening, thinks Alex as she sits pretending to be utterly fascinated by the lecture Peet is providing for her on the fourteenth century English Church's attitudes towards women. There's definitely a strange sound behind her, very faint, like a thin angry mosquito whine, combined with a sort of irregular low breathing sound. The light in the class-

room as a whole is slowly changing, getting brighter. Even Peet notices.

4   I'm not a very imaginative person really. You know what I mean; I like to escape with a novel now and again, and I definitely enjoy a good horror video, but this, well this was different. It was a very ordinary sort of day, raining (as always), and it was Monday, so that meant Chaucer. Pretty boring stuff on the whole, apart from the rude bits. Well, anyway, something happened on that day which I suppose I can only call a supernatural occurrence. (Sorry about the long words!) There was something in the corner of the classroom, that's all. The lesson was dragging on as usual, and then there was something. I'm sorry that I can't be clearer than that. Something just 'arrived' into the room. I know this sounds crazy, and I've already told you that I'm a very unimaginative kind of person, but, well, it appeared to me like one of those hologram things and it looked just like, well, an angel. It had wings, very tall thin ones sort of folded up, made of feathers, and the whole thing was a sort of golden colour. You could see the door through it at first and then slowly it became more solid and so, clearer. And you know, the strangest thing was that it had an incredibly wrinkled old face. You always imagine angels as being in their twenties or something . . . Well, you do, don't you?

5   Doesn't it rain in this county? Sometimes you think you'd better start building youself an ark, forty cubits by sixteen cubits. It'd have to be big. Wood? Glass fibre these days probably. Couldn't really take all the animals – too many. Why did Noah allow mosquitoes and wasps on board anyway? Odd. That sounds like a mosquito – thin faint whine they make. No. Can't be. Wrong time of the year. Where do they go in Autumn? Hide under the carpets? Hibernate? Die? Emigrate south then, as swallow food? Hotter climates. Flotillas of them in the air, heading for Africa. Armadas for Africa. How do they know south? Compasses in their heads somehow. Hang on. There's that noise again. It's in the room. Here. Not in my head. What?

Has anyone else noticed yet? I'll wait until someone else says something. Old man with wings on his back? Covered in gold leaf? How do they do that?

6   Angel 473 here. Beam me back up please. Someone's made a cock-up again. I thought He said that we weren't to be manifested in front of mortals any more. It frightens them. I haven't done this sort of thing since the Old Testament days. I seem to be in some kind of prison. Most of the prisoners are young, and have to wear tight breeches made of thick blue cloth, some of it very faded. There's a time malfunction here. The Chief Warder and the prisoners are all wearing twentieth century clothing, and yet the Chief Warder is reading out fourteenth century stuff. I'm no good with this sort of confusion. They know that up there. It's their fault. I put in for retirement last week. I've done my four thousand years, haven't I?

It's a rather silly story, granted, but it will do to demonstrate that there is a range of different narrative methods available to anyone to wants to write fiction. The kind of narrative technique that writers choose will usually depend on two things: the kind of fiction they want to produce, and the relationship they seek to establish between themselves and the reader. It's a very practical business, and something you will have to think about if you're contemplating being a writer.

Look back at passages 1, 2 and 3. They are all written in the third person (the characters are all referred to as he, she, they, or by name). This is a very common narrative method, and writers like it because 'third person narrative' fits rather well with the 'omniscient' point of view (with which the author gives himself godlike powers.) The narrator of passage 2, for example, can travel miles in an instant (' . . . at the eastern edge of the Atlantic Ocean, huge, grey and magnificent waves were rolling towards the Cornish coast . . . '); or get inside characters' heads and listen to what they are thinking. An omniscient narrator can also be very 'visible' and intrusive as in passage 1, which uses the old 'Dear Reader' approach addressing the reader directly. This cosy style of narrative was quite commonplace among certain eighteenth century novelists, who, for various reasons, wanted to establish a relationship with the reader in order to comment upon their fictional characters and the events that befell them. It is probably because this particular narrative technique goes back such a long way that it now seems old-fashioned or maybe artificial. (However, this kind of narrative device has had a revival in recent years.) The most interesting and odd thing about it, though, is this: that the 'narrator' who 'speaks' to us from the page isn't really the actual author of the piece. Look at passage 1 again: no real, flesh-and-blood author would speak like that – it's an assumed voice, a pretence. In other words, the old codger whose voice we hear is himself a fictitious character, every bit as fictitious as the characters he describes. In this instance, the narrator is not the writer, he's one of the cast. (Critics call him the author's persona.) The classic example of this kind of narrating persona is the 'Author' of Henry Fielding's *Tom Jones* (published in 1749). This person frequently interrupts the story to comment, to explain or to apologise to the reader for bits we might find offensive or far-fetched. But although this polite intruder calls himself The Author, he's not Henry Fielding.

Most modern novelists consider that this 'buttonholing', Dear Reader approach to narrative is awkward and rather patronising: they feel that their readers should be able to interpret and evaluate what they are reading without the assistance (or interference) of a 'visible' or foregrounded narrator. But the absence of a guide, or visible narrator, does not mean that the reader is freed from the author's control. All novelists are in the manipulation game, especially those who assume the godlike powers of the omniscient narrator. Writers who remain 'invisible' in their novels are being just as manipulative as the eighteenth century writers – Fielding, say, or Laurence Sterne – who use visible narrators; it's just that they're doing it in a more subtle and indirect way.

Most omniscient narrators confine themselves to the past tense: 'Mr Peet stood at the front of the class and opened his dull brown copy . . . ' It is perfectly possible, though, for a writer to use the present tense instead, as in passage 3: 'The light in the classroom as a whole is slowly changing . . . ' The use of the present tense makes the events seem more 'present' (obviously enough): we, the readers, are 'in' the book at the same time as the characters, so that, in a sense, we share their experiences in a more direct way; the illusion is that we witness events, rather than being informed about them retrospectively – it's a 'live' recording, so to speak. Quite a few novelists also go in for switching unobtrusively from one tense to another so as to achieve dramatic effects or changes of viewpoint. To write a whole novel in the present tense is quite a different matter. A novel written totally in the present tense can become tiresomely urgent, like someone thrusting his face right up to yours at a party in order to tell you about himself. Nevertheless, some writers have written novels in this way, and it can be an effective device for conveying what they see as the empty, relentless, humdrum routine of modern life:

Mr Bleek wakes up and goes to the office. He feeds his number into the security lock by the main door and begins his day. He climbs the stairs. The lift is out of order. He sits down at his desk and switches on his PC; it glows greenly at him. He stares greenly back.

Quite apart from the power and the freedom it gives the writer, a novelist's omniscience has certain psychological effects upon the reader. To put it simply, it's reassuring; it gives the reader some sort of security. In the company of an omniscient narrator, we can feel assured that, no matter how mysterious and chaotic his world and its inhabitants might at first appear to be, he knows what to make of them. He will explain and clarify, and perhaps finally give the whole business some kind of completeness and meaning that we can grasp and which will resolve our confusion. In earlier, more optimistic times, writers often seemed to believe that real life was like that: that as human beings progressed towards greater knowledge and wisdom, we would eventually be able to make sense of the world and live more securely in it, that the Great Novelist in the sky would reveal all, in the end. Most modern writers cannot bring themselves to subscribe to this optimism, and many of us see ourselves as living not in a world of ever-increasing clarity, but in a quarrelsome global village surrounded by a threatening darkness. This being so, an increasing number of modern writers seem to feel that it would be misleading – or downright dishonest – to pretend that a single human being, who happens to be a writer, can adopt an omniscient, explanatory role. Instead, the way they write and the way they structure their novels suggest that there can only be partial, subjective glimpses of the world: clues, not satisfying solutions.

Writers who feel this way are often attracted to a more limited narrative viewpoint: that of the fictional narrator taking part in the events of the plot. This is, after all, the narrative method most of us employ when talking about ourselves – although we describe what happens to us personally, rather than employ a fictitious character to do it for us. (This is not quite so clear-cut as it might appear, however. Most of us, let's admit it, tend to 'embroider' or dramatise the stories we tell about our past experiences, or edit out bits that are embarrassing. When we do this, we are, in a small way, fictionalising; and thus the 'I' that stars in these stories is at least partly fictitious.) This is commonly known as 'first person narrative', and passage 4 is written in this way: 'I'm not a very imaginative kind of person . . . ' The disadvantages of this narrative technique should be clear enough: if you are a fictional character *and* the narrator, both participating in and commenting upon the events that take place, then you cannot plausibly leap into the minds of the other characters; and as a physical being you are confined to the normal restrictions of time and space. You cannot, for example, fly out of that classroom to observe the waves rolling in on the Cornish coast. The first person narrative method looks, at first, to be impossibly inflexible, especially if compared to the omniscient narrative that we have been discussing. But part of the joy of writing in the first person lies in the demands it makes upon the writer's ingenuity. There are all sorts of tricks a writer can use to get round the limitations it might seem to impose – and without resorting to crude devices like telepathy and time machines. But let's look first at the advantages of first person narration. These are fairly subtle.

The garrulous narrator of passage 4 demonstrates some of the strengths of having the story-teller as a participant in the story. Here is a character whom the novelist can explore and develop in great depth – but without seeming to. His personality and his experiences can be portrayed not from the outside but by the character himself, 'from the inside'. The writer can exploit the possibilities of his narrator's vernacular speaking voice, and he can create the illusion of greater immediacy and dramatic impact by telling the story through someone who is actually 'there'. A fictional narrator like this can be a liar, a fool, or mad; he can have an axe to grind or a bee in his bonnet. In such cases, the reader has lots of scope to question or disbelieve or interpret the narrator's version of events. In other words, the reader gets to participate more actively in the working out of the novel. But as we said, this is a fairly subtle business. Let's imagine that the narrator of passage 4 has something strange about him – let's imagine that he is an escapee from an institution for the criminally insane passing himself off as a student (maybe there's one in your class), and that what he tells us is not, therefore, strictly true. How would we get to know that he is lunatic and how would we re-assess what he says? In other words, if the narrator is unreliable or partial or dishonest, and we reinterpret his words from a more 'superior' point of view, where does this superior perception of what is actually going on come from? Do we bring it with us, sort of 'ready-made', when we begin the novel? Or is it something that the author secretly conveys? If all we have to go on is what this dodgy narrator tells us, how is it that we can somehow learn to doubt him? One thing worth remembering is that we can learn as much from what is not said as we can from what is.

But, yes, as a narrative technique, the first person is limiting. So how do writers get out of the trap of being restricted to only one consciousness? One of the most famous of all American novels is Scott Fitzgerald's *The Great Gatsby*, which is told in the first person by one of its characters, Nick Carraway. The book is full of ingenious techniques that enable Fitzgerald's narrator to travel in time and space and get inside the heads of the other characters. Carraway doesn't have to be telepathic, just a good listener. Most of the people he meets are either unhappy or drunk (or both) and consequently feel the need to confide in him, which they very frequently do. His readiness to listen means that we readers can also, via Carraway, 'listen in' and find out from others about incidents that he himself could not possibly have witnessed. We get inside the heads of other characters because, whenever Nick is around, they blurt out their innermost feelings and desires, and reveal their opinions of the other characters in the novel. Sometimes Fitzgerald sidesteps the problems of first person narrative by using the breathtakingly simple and fraudulent device of conjecture. Here is Nick Carraway describing the unknowable thoughts of a man (Gatsby) who, for reasons of plot (he is just about to be murdered), has to be alone:

He must have looked up at an unfamiliar sky through frightening leaves and shivered as he found what a grotesque thing a rose is and how raw the sunlight was upon the scarcely created grass.

F. Scott Fitzgerald: The Great Gatsby

Just look at what an immense amount of work the words 'He must have' do in that sentence, and what an outrageous cheat it is. You have to be good to get away with that sort of thing: in this case, the startling adjectives 'frightening', 'grotesque', 'raw' and 'scarcely' deflect our attention from the trick that Fitzgerald is playing on us which is, of course, that Nick Carraway could not have known what Gatsby was feeling.

Passage 5 (have another look) is an example of a narrative technique which is often called 'stream of consciousness'. This kind of narrative attempts to mimic the constant and random thoughts that rush through our minds during our waking (and maybe sleeping) hours. It is a very twentieth-century narrative method. There is some doubt about who first 'invented' it, although a novelist called Dorothy Richardson was probably the first to explore its potential. Most literary people would direct you to better-known writers like James Joyce, Virginia Woolf and William Faulkner for examples of this style of writing. What stream of consciousness narrative suggests is that the human mind is constantly busy with a kind of associative chatter which is almost incoherent to anyone other than the thinker. And this means that stream of consciousness narrative is very far 'in there', very subjective and partial: it is at the other end of the scale from the omniscient point of view. The advantages of the technique are that the writer can create an absorbing intimacy between the reader and a character's innermost thoughts and obsessions, and we readers (if we are so inclined) can have some fun 'ordering' and making connections between what are apparently disorderly thoughts and images. The disadvantage is that for the reader it is such wretchedly hard work, and very few of us have the stamina to struggle through more than a page or two of this sort of jumbly stuff – which is why only about six people have ever read James Joyce's *Finnegan's Wake*, even though thousands claim to have done so.

Passage 6 gives us the panicky thoughts of the angel himself (or herself – the gender of angels is never too easy to determine). Like passages 4 and 5 it is an 'interior monologue'; but unlike the stream of consciousness 'garble' of passage 5 it consists of more or less coherent sentences – it is silent speech, rather than a transcript of disorderly thought-processes. And it differs from passage 4 because it is written from what is sometimes called the 'Martian' viewpoint. A good many writers now and in the past have got mileage and amusement out of this technique. It involves using a narrator who is an alien or outsider, and who therefore misunderstands and misinterprets everything around him – often in a bewildered and comic way. It isn't necessary to have your narrator an alien or an angel, either: in a novel called *Other People*, Martin Amis shows us the world through the eyes of a woman who has lost her memory, and she describes everyday objects and activities in a bizarre, un-comprehending way. We read passage 6 confident in our superior knowledge that colleges are not really prisons, that wearing denim is not compulsory, that students are not prisoners and that teach-ers are not warders. Because this divine visitor is from outside our culture, he misinterprets what is, to us, obvious. Consequently, the Martian narrative is rich in irony: it enables a writer to exploit comi-cally the gap between what the narrator thinks he sees and what we know he is 'really' seeing. But, as is usually the case with irony, the effects of this can be quite subtle. At first, the reader is presented with little puzzles, or riddles – what are these blue cloth breeches? – and so forth. But then the Martian view starts to challenge our com-placent view of our own world – interpretations that seem naïve or ignorant become satirical. Perhaps our educational system does 'imprison' the minds of those who are 'confined' within it. Perhaps students are rigidly conformist in their choice of clothes (there's no shortage of fashion victims in my college). And perhaps the way we do things, and the way our society is organised and controlled is not natural or inevitable at all. In challenging our comfortable or lazy assumptions, the Martian viewpoint can be the most subversive nar-rative technique of all.

So much for our Angel in the Classroom story. We have not, of course, covered all the available narrative techniques – and if we tried to do so we'd be here all day. We should, though, say a word or two about one ancient and important literary form, the epistolatory novel: the novel, that is, which is written in the form of letters ex-changed between its characters. One of the first great eighteenth cen-tury novelists, Samuel Richardson, used this technique in a number of his works. As with the first person narrative, the epistolatory narrator is limited by place and time, and the reader is confined to being in one head at a time. But a fictional correspondent can write many different letters to several different characters, and in this way reveal a variety of relationships; and such letters will, of course, undergo modulations of tone and language depending on to whom they are addressed. The furtive reading of other people's letters is something many of us enjoy but few of us would admit to; reading an epistolary novel is a guilt-free way of indulging in this less than admirable desire to snoop. This may be one reason why this long-established narrative method remains popular, as the more recent success of Alice Walker's *The Color Purple* demonstrates.

Write your own story

The best way to investigate the possibilities of different kinds of narrative technique is for you to try them for yourself. Have a go at it. Here are six basic plot situations. Choose one and then write at least four paragraphs, each one using a different narrative approach, until you complete the plot-line of your story.

1 An old man or woman reminisces about the past.
2 A child witnesses a murder.
3 A student returns home to find that his/her furniture can talk.
4 A ventriloquist tries to claim Unemployment Benefit for his/her dummy.
5 A crazed poet tries to assassinate the star of a soap-opera.
6 Three astronauts discover that their on-board computer is disobeying them.

Feel free to adopt, adapt or ignore the six kinds of narrative used in our tale of the angel. When you have written your story, ask yourself which of the narrative techniques you used felt the most comfortable to you, and with which one you consider you were the most successful. (The chances are that they will be one and the same, but they may not be.) Then ask yourself why this particular approach worked best. Was it because it just came naturally to

you, or was it because something about the nature of the story de-
manded that kind of technique? Or were there other more subtle
reasons?

The private eye

We're going to look next at two particular species of narrative
fiction – detective stories and crime novels.

For a short while, one of the writers of this book worked as
a mobile librarian, squeezing a vanload of culture through the
lanes of deepest Devon, providing the locals with, sometimes,
the works of Jane Austen and Joseph Conrad, but more often –
much more often – with bales of what is often called 'genre fiction'.
Genre fiction is written to a specific kind of formula or pattern,
and its subdivisions can be quite extensive and precise. It wouldn't
do to offer the inhabitants of Cheriton Fitzpaine Romances:
they would want Hospital Romances, while the more bloodthirsty populace of Sampford Peverell would demand War
Romances.

Genre novels are usually classified by subject: the Western, Science Fiction, Horror, Occult, and – most popular of all – Detective
Stories and Crime Fiction. It's probably best to start by making
a few distinctions between detective fiction and crime fiction. Most
readers of detective stories are interested primarily in playing the
'whodunnit' game, to discover whether it really was the butler
who knocked off Mrs Bumbleby-Scott, and to find this out before
the detective does. A variation on the whodunnit is the howdunnit,
where it is the method of the murder, rather than the identity which
is the issue. Conventionally, the identity, motives and method of
the criminal are revealed in an often tiresome exposition towards the end of the story. Like all games, detective fiction has
to obey certain rules. The writer must provide his readers with
clues, the culprit's methods must seem more or less plausible,
the detective cannot employ supernatural powers to snare the

killer, and so on. In that sense, detective novels cannot disregard the rules of physical reality in the way that fairy stories, say, can; yet the way they are constructed and the way they operate are just as much bound by genre convention. The characters in detective stories are frequently as melodramatically two-dimensional as those who populate fairy stories, and in both these kinds of story-telling it is the plot that is of greatest importance. A detective story which delved into the complexities of the criminal mind, or which explored the the more mysterious areas of human relationships would cease to be a 'real' detective story as far as traditional readers are concerned, and would be returned very grumpily to the mobile library.

Writers of detective fiction are an orthodox bunch when it comes to narrative method. They tend to choose either the omniscient third person narrator (who, of necessity, has to spend much of his time withholding information from the reader) or, just as commonly, the first person narrator – often the detective himself or a close acquaintance (like Holmes' good friend Dr Watson). First person narrative works very well in this genre, because it allows the writer to disguise the story as an autobiographical reminscence or 'case study'. The originators of detective fiction include some famous names: Edgar Allen Poe *(The Murders in the Rue Morgue)*, Charles Dickens *(The Mystery of Edwin Drood)*, Wilkie Collins *(The Moonstone)* and, of course, Sherlock Holmes' creator, Conan Doyle. The Golden Age of English detective fiction was probably the 1920s and 30s, when writers such as Dorothy Sayers, Agatha Christie, John Dickinson Carr and Ellery Queen provided their readers with hundreds of ingenious fictional puzzles to solve.

Classic English detective fiction tends to be populated by middle-class characters living relatively prosperous lives in a society which is both stable and highly stratified. Crime is a very real threat to the status quo, the stability and security of this social world. Villains, are frequently subversive in that they can imitate the dress, speech and behaviour of those they prey upon; the detective (often an amateur and often an upper-class gent) is therefore in the business of apprehending these bounders so that social order can be restored. (This is, after all, what the word 'order' means in the phrase 'law and order'.)

Here's a fairly typical and relatively modern example of the detective genre. These are the opening paragraphs of a short story. Questions follow.

In a first-floor office in Hatton Garden two men sat at separate tables, silent, almost motionless, each one staring fixedly in front of him – doing nothing. In one corner of the room a small but very modern safe had been let into the wall; it now stood open, as did the four drawers at the bottom of it; the thoughts of the two occupants of the room were concentrated upon that safe, and for the last twenty minutes, after a spate of furious argument, they had not spoken to one another. Apart from the distant rumble of Holborn traffic the ticking of the clock alone broke the silence.

Except for a similarity of well-made, sombre clothing, and certain unmistakable racial characteristics, the two men were utterly unlike each other; the elder was short, fat, and grey; the younger, tall, thin and black; they were, in fact, unrelated, but for nearly thirty years they had been intimate friends – until today.

Footsteps sounded on the stairs, a knock; a small boy ushered in a young man in a dark blue suit carrying a bowler hat.

'Detective-Inspector Poole, New Scotland Yard,' said the new-comer. 'You're Levi, Berg and Phillips, gentlemen? I'm instucted that you asked for an officer to be sent round?'

Instantly the two partners burst into a torrent of speech, stopped, and glared at one another. Inspector Poole recognised the situation at a glance.

'Perhaps it would be more convenient if I took your statements separately, gentlemen,' he said.

After a moment's struggle to control his raging suspicions the thin Mr Berg retired and the stout Mr Levi burst into his tale.

'We are diamond merchants,' he said. 'We have been in partnership, Aaron Berg and I, for thirty years. For the last fifteen we have had another partner, George Phillips, who brought capital into the business when things were bad – in the war, when Aaron, who is a German, was interned. Phillips brought his young brother into the business too, a few years ago, but not as a partner – as a clerk.'

'He is here now – your partner, Mr Phillips?' asked Poole.

'He and his brother have gone away for the Easter holidays; they went last night.'

'Leaving you and Mr Berg in charge?'

'Yes; we do not need a holiday at Easter; we are not Christians.'

Mr Levi spoke with quiet dignity; the detective felt an unreasonable inclination to blush.

'In the ordinary course of business,' continued Mr Levi, 'we keep in that safe diamonds, cut and uncut, to a value of from five thousand to twenty thousand pounds at a time. Lately we have been negotiating a big sale and we have had some fine uncut stones of unusual value. When we locked the safe last night there were in it stones to the value of more than 30,000 pounds. This afternoon there are . . . none.'

The old man's flabby jowl quivered with emotion.

'You say the safe was locked last night, sir; who locked it?'

With a gesture of his pudgy hand, Mr Levi indicated that he would explain everything – in his own way.

'The safe has three keys, two of which open the door and one which opens the drawers – in which the diamonds are kept; the body of the safe only holds ledgers and important papers. Berg and Phillips each have key of the door, I alone have the key of the drawers – but I have not a key of the door. Once the drawers and safe have been locked, the diamonds can only be reached if both Berg and I or Phillips and I are present. The keys never leave our possession; we never give them to anyone else to open the safe or the drawers; the holder of the key, alone operates it. That is the only way to be safe.'

The Detective, his eyes on the empty safe, reflected that even this system did not appear to be infallible.

Henry Wade: The Three Keys

1 What sort of narrative technique is this, and why might it be an appropriate one for this story?
2 How does the first paragraph try to grab the reader's attention? (You might consider the syntax and the rhythm of that first sentence, as well as the way those small details signal particular kinds of relevant information.)
3 Characterisation in detective fiction tends be relatively uncomplicated. What sort of information are we given about the three characters here, and how are we provided with it?
    The Jewish diamond merchants seem to come very close, at times, to being 'racial stereotypes'. What is racial stereotyping, and how would it be likely to affect our reading of this story?
4 From the sentence beginning 'We are diamond merchants . . . ', our interest is focussed not on the characters or the relationships between them, but on a totally different matter: what?
5 The function of this writer's prose is, on the whole, to be transparent and to be an efficient conveyor of information. What is interesting about the sentence which begins 'Except for . . . ' and the paragraph beginning with 'The safe has three keys . . . '?
6 What would you suggest is the ultimate purpose of this story?

A greyer area

The social world of the crime novel tends to be rather different to that of the detective novel. This next extract should make the distinction clear enough.

I have a client named Teddy Franklin. Teddy Franklin is a car thief. He is thirty-two years old, and he is one of the best car thieves on the Eastern seaboard. Cadillac Ted is so good that he is able to support himself as a car thief. He has been arrested repeatedly, which is how he made my acquaintance, but he has never done time. That is because I am so good. It is also because Teddy is so good.

Teddy is as cute as a shithouse rat. He is an expert. He never leaves any prints. He never does anything in the presence of unreliable people who might turn out to be witnesses for the prosecution. He does not become attached to any of the cars he steals, but unloads them within an hour or so of the instant that he steals them. If you have a car with a kill switch cutting out the ignition, and Teddy wants your car, he will have it started within thirty seconds of the time that he spots your car. If you have a car with a hidden burglar alarm, Teddy will have that alarm disabled before it has even gone off. If you have a crook lock, a steel bar immobilising the steering wheel and brake, he will remove it inside a minute – I do not know how Teddy does this, but Teddy assures me that he does do it, and I'm sure he does have some professional secrets. The only device that Teddy admits to be sufficient to defeat him is the invention that shuts off the gas and the ignition and seals the hood shut so that Teddy cannot get at the wires and jump them.

'I dunno,' Teddy said, 'I don't think I can beat that one. Short of taking a torch to it, I don't think I can do it. I tried a couple of times, just for the hell of it. Didn't even have an order for that particular car, but I saw the sticker that said it had one of those things, and sure enough it worked. 'Course when the owner got back, he wasn't goin' nowhere in it neither, which is something, because if I need a torch to get into it, so does the guy who's got a right to get into it. I imagine the only way you could take one of those things is if you backed the wrecker up to it and towed the damned thing off to some place where you could work on it.'

George V. Higgins: Kennedy for the Defense

Clearly, we are more than a million miles from the polite drawing-rooms of English detective fiction with their decanters of poisoned sherry on the sideboard. This 'hard-boiled' prose style owes a lot to the founding fathers of American crime fiction, namely Dashiell Hammet, James M. Cain and Raymond Chandler. The first two wrote their best-known novels in the 1930s, Chandler mostly in the 40s and 50s. George V. Higgins has written several novels which continue this great tradition. Try reading that short piece again and answering the following questions:

1 The narrator of this novel (Kennedy) is a lawyer, not a detective. How does this affect his attitude towards criminals and criminal behaviour? Where do his sympathies lie? What words or phrases in the passage provide you with clues?

2 What kind of relationship is Kennedy establishing with the reader in the first paragraph?

3 Why, do you suppose, does Higgins make his narrator begin his sentences with similar patterns of words in the second paragraph?

4 What are the advantages of using this kind of narrative technique over the omniscient narrator method? What are the bonuses that Higgins gets by using a first person narrator here?

The language of this extract is not standard British English, and the moral values displayed by the lawyer-narrator are distinctly not those that you would find in that comfortable and assured world so ably defended by the detective heroes of earlier English novels. The social world of the American crime novel has morals and values that are a gritty grey in colour, and it is a world which the narrator often distrusts or despises. In American cities the streets are mean and the cops are not people from whom you would ask directions or the time of day.

The first person narrative is obviously crucial in this passage because it's a fast, no-messing-about way of getting across the personality and the attitudes of the central character who is also the narrator. The no-nonsense style reflects the nature of the man. The vocabulary is aggressively vernacular, the tone is forceful and the language is almost totally literal (look at the effect of that one start-ling simile). But it is worth noting how, for all its energetic rhythms, the language is highly stylised, which should suggest to us that the world of the crime novel is just as artificial as that of the traditional detective novel, even though the criminals do shoot and stab rather than resort to more elaborate forms of homicide involving obscure poisons. The modern crime novel does not usually set the reader puzzles to solve (a Higgins story is as likely to begin with the capture of a murderer). But, if you think about it, all readers and writers of fiction are involved in a 'game' because there is always some kind of understanding about what the rules and conventions are. When we declare that a novel is 'good' we are perhaps saying that the novelist has 'won' (won us over, won our admiration). It's an important part of being a good critical reader to understand the rules and conven-tions of the game, and how different kinds (or genres) of fiction will have different sets of rules. (We do not expect from science fiction the same 'logic', for example, that we expect from detective fiction.)

The private I

It would be wrong to think that the 'rules and conventions' of a par-ticular genre are a self-imposed handicap for the writer. Quite the opposite is true: they are a means to an end. They allow the writer to give a recognisable shape to a story. The conventions of the detective, crime or spy novel can also be a means to an end for writers whose aims and intentions differ from or transcend those usually associated with the genre. Authors whom we like to think of as 'serious' writers (Joseph Conrad and Graham Greene, for examples) have adopted the manners of the spy novel for their own ends. One reason for this is that the detective, the private eye and the spy easily lend themselves to symbolic interpretation. They are all observers, they are all concerned with finding The Truth, they try to penetrate and make sense of the mystery and confusion of the world. And many, or most, of us feel the need to do this with regard to our own lives at some time or another. One of the great attractions and pleasures of the detective story is that when the hero 'cracks the case' it reassures us that it is possible to solve the mysteries of life. In fact, it is even reassuring if the hero fails, because if the Ace Investigator cannot make sense of it all, then it's not so depressing if we can't either. Another possible reason why 'serious' writers are attracted to detectives and spies is that such characters resemble writers in certain ways. Writers and detectives are both in the business of observing and investigating and looking for clues as to the reasons behind human behaviour; and both are inclined to see themselves as outsiders. The private eye is perhaps a natural alter ego for a writer.

With these possibilities in mind, we'll end this chapter with a brief look at some passages from a novel by the American writer Paul Auster, who has employed some of the conventions of the crime and detective story for his own rather peculiar but fascinating purposes. Auster's book *The New York Trilogy* features private eyes who are employed by often anonymous clients; and often their job is to watch apparently innocent people. Here is what Quinn, one of Auster's protagonists, thinks about private eye novels and the kind of desperate searching for meanings that distinguish both the sleuth and the writer:

What he liked about these books was their sense of plenitude and economy. In the good mystery there is nothing wasted, no

sentence, no word that is not significant. And even if it is not significant, it has the potential to be so – which amounts to the same thing. The world of the book comes to life, seething with possibilities, with secrets and contradictions. Since everything seen or said, even the slightest, most trivial thing, can bear a connection to the outcome of the story, nothing must be overlooked. Everything becomes essence; the center of the book shifts with each event that propels it forward. The center, then, is everywhere, and no circumference can be drawn until the book has come to its end.

The detective is the one who looks, who listens, who moves through this morass of objects and events in search of the thought, the idea, that will pull all these things together and make sense of them. In effect, the writer and the detective are interchangeable. The reader sees the world through the detective's eye, experiencing the proliferation of its details as if for the first time. He has become awake to the things around him, as if they might speak to him, as if, because of the attentiveness he now brings to them, they might begin to carry a meaning other than the simple fact of their existence. Private eye. The term held a triple meaning for Quinn. Not only was it the letter 'i', standing for 'investigator', it was 'I' in the upper case, the tiny life-bud buried in the body of the breathing self. At the same time, it was also the physical eye of the writer, the eye of the man who looks out from himself into the world and demands that the world reveal itself to him.

Paul Auster: The New York Trilogy

Quinn is clearly in trouble here, as is anyone who starts to lose sight of the distinction between life and fiction. It is true that in detective fiction it is often the indiscriminate close observation of tiny details that solves mysteries. But as human beings we cannot survive that way – we have to be discriminating in the way we see things. If everything around us was constantly signalling information to us, we would quickly be unable to see anything at all, and drown in confusion. Quinn, who seems to want to be an all-seeing, all-knowing eye, is heading for trouble, maybe for madness. He is called out on a case to meet a Mr Stillman, and as soon as he enters Stillman's apartment Auster again takes up the theme of seeing and perception:

> **As he crossed the threshold and entered the apartment, he could feel himself going blank, as if his brain had suddenly shut off. He had wanted to take in the details of what he was seeing, but the task was somehow beyond him at that moment. The apartment loomed up around him as a kind of blur. He realized that it was large, perhaps five or six rooms, and that it was richly furnished, with numerous art objects, silver ashtrays, and elaborately framed pictures on the walls. But that was all. No more than a general impression – even though he was there, looking at those things with his own eyes.**
>
> *Paul Auster: The New York Trilogy*

We spend most of our lives, probably, forming such 'general impressions' of the world; it's one of the great survival processes we are equipped to perform, and no-one could possibly do otherwise in, say, a supermarket or a library. This is, quite naturally, what Quinn does when he goes into Stillman's apartment. What is unusual is Quinn's dismay when he does it; he wants more: he wants to do what he thinks a detective in a detective novel should do, which is take in everything in detail. He's beginning to think that he may not be up to the part that his creator has lumbered him with. But if Quinn thinks he might be having an identity crisis, it's nothing compared with the one that the mysterious Stillman is going through. The meeting between Quinn and Stillman is highly ironic: here we have a private eye who is none too sure that he is one, confronted by someone who doesn't seem sure that he exists at all:

Everything about Peter Stillman was white. White shirt, open at the neck; white pants, white shoes, white socks. Against the pallor of his skin, the flaxen thinness of his hair, the effect was almost transparent, as though one could see through to the blue veins behind the skin of his face. This blue was almost the same as the blue of his eyes: a milky blue that seemed to dissolve into a mixture of sky and clouds. Quinn could not imagine himself addressing a word to this person. It was as though Stillman's presence was a command to be silent.

Stillman settled slowly into his chair and at last turned his attention to Quinn. As their eyes met, Quinn suddenly felt that Stillman had become invisible. He could see him sitting in the chair across from him, but at the same time it felt as though he was not there. It occurred to Quinn that perhaps Stillman was blind. But no, that did not seem possible. The man was looking at him, even studying him, and if recognition did not flicker across his face, it still held something more than a blank stare. Quinn did not know what to do. He sat there dumbly in his seat, looking back at Stillman. A long time passed.

'No questions, please,' the young man said at last. 'Yes. No. Thank you.' He paused for a moment. 'I am Peter Stillman. I say this of my own free will. Yes. That is not my real name. No. Of course, my mind is not all it should be. But nothing can be done about that. No. About that. No, no. Not anymore.

'You sit there and think: who is this person talking to me? What are these words coming from his mouth? I will tell you. Or else I will not tell you. My mind is not all it should be. I say this of my own free will. But I will try. Yes and no. I will try to tell you, even if my mind makes it hard. Thank you.

'My name is Peter Stillman. Perhaps you have heard of me, but more than likely not. No matter. That is not my real name. My real name I cannot remember. Excuse me. Not that it makes a difference. That is to say, anymore.

'This is what is called speaking. I believe that is the term. When words come out, fly into the air, live for a moment and die. Strange, is it not? I myself have no opinion. No and no again. But still, there are words you will need to have. There are many of them. Many millions I think. Perhaps only three or four. Excuse me. But I am doing well today. So much better than usual. If I can give you the words you need to have, it will be a great victory. Thank you. Thank you a million times over.

'Long ago there was mother and father. I remember none of that. They say: mother died. Who they are I cannot say. Excuse me. But that is what they say.

'No mother then. Ha ha. Such is my laughter now, my belly burst of mumbo jumbo. Ha ha ha. Big father said: it makes no difference. To me. That is to say, to him. Big father of the big muscles and the boom, boom, boom. No questions now, please.

'I say what they say because I know nothing. I am only poor Peter Stillman, the boy who can't remember. Boo hoo. Willy nilly. Nincompoop. Excuse me. They say, they say. But what does poor little Peter say? Nothing, nothing. Anymore.

'There was this. Dark. Very dark. As dark as very dark. They say: that was the room. As if I could talk about it. The dark, I mean. Thank you.

'Dark, dark. They say for nine years. Not even a window. Poor Peter Stillman.'

Paul Auster: The New York Trilogy

As in all classic detective stories, we are here presented with a puzzle; but this time the puzzle is a matter of who? rather than who-dunnit? The mystery that Quinn is confronting here is a really big one: what is a human being? As Peter Stillman's rather allegorical name implies, he seems to have all the outward appearances of a member of the human race, but he seems to be seriously lacking in some of the qualifications you need to be a full member. Answering the following questions may help you to decide whether or not Stillman is still a man:

1 **What is the significance of the colour of Stillman's clothing and the colour of his eyes?**

2 **What are the social skills that Stillman seems to lack?**

3 **Stillman's language is, of course, most peculiar. But what is different about it compared to normal human language?**

4 **Stillman has a rather 'Martian' view of the nature of words and language. What is it?**

5 **Play the detective for a moment: is there anything significant about Stillman's last few remarks? Are there clues there that might explain something?**

6 **Stillman repeatedly refers to free will, memory and opinion – saying that he has the first but not the other two. Do you believe him, on either count? Why, do you think, does he harp on these things? How are they relevant to our concept of human identity?**

The last part of that last question gets us into deep waters, and nobody could reasonably expect you to come up with a complete answer. Philosophers and writers seem to agree that there isn't one. Yet these things – free will, memory and opinion (or judgement) do seem to be essential components in the 'package' we call human identity. If Stillman lacks them, does that mean he is not 'one of us'? And where does Quinn go from here? You'll have to read *The New York Trilogy* to find out.

One of the things that Paul Auster's books imply – and one of the things that we have been getting at in this chapter – is that the way we see things is the same thing as the way we understand things. 'See' and 'understand' are sometimes synonymous, if you 'see' what we mean. And seeing is not a passive receiving of objective images: we make choices about what we see, and in so doing impose meanings on the world. In choosing a particular narrative technique, a writer is choosing a position, and in so doing is imposing a certain view or version of the world on us, the readers. Which is to say that narrative is much more than just a way of telling a story.

SECTION
FOUR

DOING ENGLISH

1

Doing English Today

What is literary theory?

New ways of reading, grouped together under the term 'literary theory', are now seen as central to university English courses. A recent survey carried out by the Council for College and University English of all university English departments in the United Kingdom revealed that four out of every five taught a compulsory first-year course on literary theory. Three-quarters thought that knowing about literary theory was essential; the remainder thought it to be desirable. *But what is it?*

Literary theory is a catch-all term for a huge range of new and different ways of reading and interpreting texts. More correctly, then, it might be called 'literary theories', since different approaches needn't agree with each other. Moving on from the 'one right way' of interpreting, these new approaches to literature reflect the different concerns and ideas of a very wide range of people, not just a (so-called) 'cultured' English elite. This means that ways of reading which were marginalised or seen as 'wrong' because of the influence of the one, traditional model of English have begun to emerge and develop. Important and influential ideas from other disciplines have entered the subject: English now draws on subjects like history, politics, women's studies, sociology, gender studies, linguistics, philosophy and so on. As you begin to explore literary theory you will no doubt hear about historicism, cultural politics, feminisms and other 'theories' that have come out of these other disciplines. New ways of reading have also developed from within the subject of English itself, in reaction to the rather narrow focus of the traditional approach to literature.

This new view of doing English is represented in Figure 1.1.

At the heart of literary theory, then, is the realisation that every way of reading brings with it presuppositions. More than this, because everyone is different there simply cannot be one correct way of reading. But how is literary theory useful?

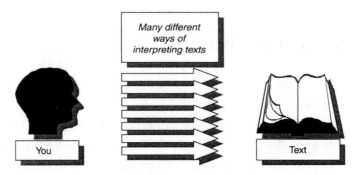

Figure 1.1 **The new view of 'doing English'.**

Using theory

This way of understanding what English is, and of understanding what you are doing when you are doing English, brings literature closer to you, the student. Those who have shaped English as a school, college and university subject have usually tried to teach about literature, art and life without admitting that the method they use takes certain ideas for granted. Often, they do not even show that English follows 'a method', assuming instead that it's 'the only way'. This often means that what you write in exams and essays about a work of literature has nothing to do with what you might really feel or think about it, which can be confusing and frustrating. To state this in formal terms, this shows the discrepancy between your location in the world and the presuppositions of the discipline of English. New approaches are trying to give more weight to different presuppositions and different ways of interpreting.

Once you've realised that interpretations are determined by world-views and that many interpretations are valid, you can begin to explore a whole array of important ideas. A key to this is remembering that you aren't limited to your own world-view: you can learn about different ways in which different people might interpret the same text. While your initial reading might be shaped by your presuppositions, literary theory offers a huge, possibly infinite, number of ways of approaching literature. You are free to choose one or another critical method, or to switch from one to the other, or to experiment with a selection. English becomes a question of reading certain sorts of texts in many different sorts of ways. There is no longer a *'right'* way to interpret literature.

What are the actual mechanics of using different approaches to literature? Any critical method works by reading with certain questions in mind. The context in which we read, our expectations and experiences, make us concentrate on certain issues when we read. These focus our reading and so structure our interpretations. For example, imagine the context for reading is that you have to answer an essay question and your expectation is that the material you need is in the text. Think about any of the novels, poems or plays you've studied. Now imagine you are asked any of these questions before you start to read: What happens in the plot here? Is this character likeable? How are metaphors being used to achieve a certain effect? Each of these three basic questions will draw your attention to different parts of the text: the plot question will make you look at events, the character question makes you concentrate on what that character says and does, the question on metaphor makes you look at how the language is woven together. By focusing your attention on different aspects of the text, the questions make you read in a different way and so lead you to different interpretations of the text. You might even ignore metaphor or plot if you are concentrating on character.

Literary theories simply offer different sorts of questions to take into a text. Feminist approaches, for example, might suggest you ask: How does this text represent the relationships between women and men? Historical approaches might lead you to ask: What is this text telling us about its historical period? The text may or may not explicitly be about these things, but you make these questions your specific focus in reading and base your interpretation on them.

You can also think about the questions that shape other people's interpretations. If you're listening to a teacher or lecturer, or reading somebody's thoughts on a work of literature, ask yourself: What unspoken questions is she or he answering? By uncovering these questions, you will learn a lot about that particular method of interpretation and about what that person thinks is really important. A greater challenge is to ask yourself what questions haven't been answered, or haven't even been raised. Once you've worked through this, you can read the text with different questions in mind, and see how different critical methods give different interpretations. Each will show up things the other methods don't.

There's no need, incidentally, to think that all these theories will agree with each other: in fact, they are more stimulating and productive when they don't. Moreover, they don't add to a 'super-theory' or a 'Grand Unifying Theory of Everything'. Each has its own way of interpreting. Indeed, to have lots of different critical approaches to texts means that we can compare and contrast them. If English is about reading texts in different sorts of ways, it is also about examining how and why we choose these ways. English is not only about *reading* literature; it's also a question of *thinking about how we read.* We can show this on our diagram, by adding another arrow representing a focus on interpretation itself. The name for this 'study of interpretation' is *hermeneutics,* which is what I've called the arrow in Figure 1.2.

The realisation that how we read is as important as what we read is perhaps the most important innovation in the study of literature in the last twenty or thirty years. It has changed English completely as a subject and given it a new burst of life. And it is this realisation that underlies the new ways of reading that are called, in a rather all-inclusive way, 'literary theory'.

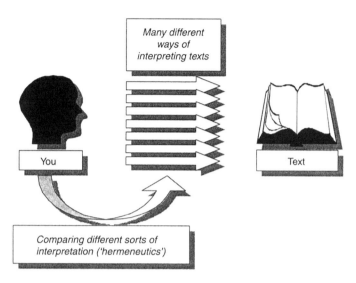

Figure 1.2 Doing English today.

What does this mean for you?

At most universities, then, studying English involves not just reading works of literature, but learning to interpret them in different ways. It also involves understanding how different ways of interpretation work, as this can reveal what other people consider to be significant about literature and central to their lives. This has the potential to create exciting new readings of texts, but also to make you think about the way you see the world and your place in it. Consciously reading from different perspectives can change your ideas about the text and even about your place in the world. In this way, the subject of English can bring to light and even challenge ideas we take for granted. Because of this, many critics and educators say that this sort of questioning and reading from other perspectives is central to doing English. I would argue that this power to make us think about ourselves and others is one of the things that makes English such a valuable subject and is why literary theory is essential to doing English.

Unfortunately, change doesn't come easily. In the last twenty or thirty years the issues raised by literary theory have caused terrible arguments and divisions between students and teachers of English in schools, colleges and universities all over the English-speaking world. In part, this has led to the gap between English in secondary and higher education. Although the situation has been changing in English in the last few years, many students trained in the traditional method of studying literature continue to search for 'the right answer'.

Summary

Doing English involves reading works of literature, learning to interpret them in different ways and understanding how these different approaches work. These new approaches have the potential to create new readings of texts and to make you think about the way you see the world and your place in it. You are, or should be, free to choose one or another method, or to experiment with a selection.

- English has changed in the last twenty years or so. These changes can be understood by looking at the issue of interpretation. When you read, you interpret. No interpretation is neutral or objective, as we are all influenced by a number of presuppositions.
- 'Literary theory' is a catch-all term for a huge range of new and different ways to read and interpret texts, reflecting the different concerns and ideas of a very wide range of people, not just a 'cultured', 'English' elite. All this encourages us to think about how we interpret.

2

Critical Attitudes

- Where should we start with thinking about how we read?
- What is the intrinsic attitude?
- What is the extrinsic attitude?

English can appear to be quite daunting once you realise that there's an infinite number of ways you can read. If you're told to explore different methods of interpretation, challenge your presuppositions and think about how you read, where are you supposed to start?

Learning about different critical approaches or theories is a *process* that you go through. A step in this process is to look for patterns in the way these critical approaches work. To do this is to look for the presuppositions behind them and to think about the contexts in which texts are understood. In this chapter I shall outline one pattern which can be used as a starting point for thinking about a wide variety of critical approaches.

Into the text or out from the text?

If you look at a painting, are you looking through a window to another world or are you simply looking at the composition of colour and shape on a flat canvas? If you see a painting as a *window*, you might be concerned with what is going on behind the window: who the people are, say, and why they had their picture painted. You might ask about the historical significance of, for example, the skull on the shelf or even why the painter chose that particular subject in the first place. If, however, a picture is only a flat canvas, then you would ask different questions: about how the tones contrast, or how the shapes relate to one another. You might just be struck by the beautiful range of colours.

This same contrast occurs in thinking about literature. When you read a novel, poem or play, how do you approach it? Do you look at it as a beautifully woven fabric of language? Or as an example of writing which tells you about the historical period in which it was written? Is it stimulating because it puts words together in a new way? Or because it pours out on paper the intense experiences and interesting ideas of a particular writer? When we do English, do we study literary works for their pure artistic merit or because they reveal things about the world and their authors? Do you think of yourself as going *into* the text for itself or coming *out from* the text to explore other issues?

One of the longest debates in English has been about whether interpretation should focus on the text as a text itself (a flat canvas) or on the text as evidence for something else, such as its historical period and its attitudes, or an author's life (a window on a world). In an influential book called *Theory of Literature*, published as long ago as 1949, two critics, René Wellek and Austin Warren, called these two contrasting positions the *intrinsic* and *extrinsic* approaches to literature. These two terms are not the names for critical approaches themselves – instead they name contrasting sorts of presuppositions, tendencies or *attitudes* taken by approaches to literary texts. This debate, because it discusses what happens when we interpret in different ways and compares different methods of interpretation, is an example of hermeneutics, the study of interpretation. Certainly the debate has become more complex since 1949, but it is a very good place to start.

Intrinsic attitudes: into the text

The intrinsic attitude is often called 'formalism' because it is concerned, above all else, with the *form* of the text, its structure and language. It assumes that there is something special and uniquely 'literary' in the way literary texts use language. Because of this, the intrinsic attitude concentrates on the language of the text as its central object, considering things like the choice of metaphors, the use of symbols, structure, style, contrasts, images, and the development of the plot, to work out what a text means. Although these forms of criticism might sound rather dull and unrewarding, following the intricate paths taken in a text and looking closely at the twists and turns of its language can produce quite remarkable readings and effects. In fact, the very intense scrutiny of the 'words on the page' can result in the most unusual and challenging interpretations of texts, as the multiple and often unclear meanings of each word are weighed up and evaluated. As you concentrate on the words themselves, their meaning becomes not clearer, but more ambiguous (or *indeterminate*). This is most obvious when looking at poetry.

For example, there is a sonnet by the English poet William Wordsworth (1770–1850) called 'Composed upon Westminster Bridge', which describes all of London, seen from the bridge at dawn, stretched out and radiant: 'Earth has not anything to show more fair' and the city 'like a garment' wears 'the beauty of the morning'. The poem finishes with these lines:

> Dear God! The very houses seem asleep
> And all that mighty heart is lying still.

The first meaning of 'lying still' is that the city is spread out, not moving, lying motionless asleep. But the word 'lying' has another meaning, of course: to lie is not to tell the truth. Perhaps the sonnet is implying that the city, *despite* all the beauty of the morning light, is *still* not telling the truth. The sunrise makes London look wonderful but really the city, 'that mighty heart', is still a den of deceit, corruption, falsehood and lies. By concentrating on the language – on the *form* of the text – two separate readings have emerged. On the one hand, London is beautiful, quiet and still in the dawn light. On the other, London *seems* beautiful, but underneath and despite all this beauty it is deceitful and corrupt. These readings are contradictory and mutually exclusive: either London is really deeply beautiful and peaceful or it's actively scheming, lying and dishonest. Which reading you choose depends on the way you interpret 'lying still'.

All ways of reading share this concentration on language to some extent, but, for the critics who tend toward the intrinsic attitude, doing English is principally a matter of looking at the words on the page with great rigour. This sort of criticism first characterised the subject of English in the 1920s and 1930s. It was first most fully outlined in I. A. Richards' book *Practical Criticism* (1929). Richards gave poems out to his students, without the poets' names, dates, or any other information that might give the students ideas about the texts outside 'the words on the page'. He asked for their responses ('practical criticism') and collected the results. He felt that this was a useful way to study what he considered to be special about literature – its 'literary-ness'. For Richards, and those he inspired, 'literary-ness' is the special sort of manipulation of language that happens, they argue, only in literature, and this is where its value, and possibly its 'moral worth', lies. This idea spread to the USA in the 1930s and 1940s and became a key presupposition of the approach to literature known as 'New Criticism'. The methods of interpretation that take this intrinsic approach for granted are often still called 'practical criticism' or 'close reading'.

This sort of intrinsic approach to literature is still very influential and important (in fact, some form of 'close reading' of texts is central to most subjects). When you are asked to do a 'practical criticism', 'write an appreciation' or 'appraisal', 'analyse the main poetic methods', pay 'close attention to meaning, language and structure', investigate the 'style' or 'narrative technique', or even 'comment on the author's skill in suggesting unspoken feelings through incident and description', you are being asked to take an intrinsic approach to literature. Even questions on character or plot, although they seem to have a wider focus, usually lead you to take this approach. Think about how you'd read a text in order to answer the following questions (typical of the 'old' A level):

- How far do you see the relationship between Hamlet and Claudius as the central conflict of the play?
- What is the function of the minor characters in the novel?
- Describe a dramatic scene from the novel and discuss its importance to the novel as a whole.

You wouldn't need any knowledge outside of the play or the novel to be able to answer the questions.

Although it might offer some interesting insights, used alone this intrinsic attitude does have blind spots and rests upon some rather large assumptions, as I outlined in the previous chapter. To recap: some critics claim that intrinsic types of criticism lead to 'objective' readings, the idea that texts can be independent of their historical, social and personal context, and that 'literary-ness' makes a text a valuable work of art, which is worth studying in its own right. However, even if you claim only to be looking at the text by itself you bring your own ideas, expectations and experiences to it. How can any judgement of worth be objective?

Extrinsic attitudes: out of the text

In contrast, extrinsic methods of interpretation take it for granted that the literary text is part of the world and rooted in its context. An extrinsic critic considers that the job of criticism is to move from the text outwards to some other, not specifically literary, object or idea. Such critics use literary texts to explore other ideas about things in the world, and in turn use other ideas to explain the literary text.

Perhaps the most important and widespread sort of extrinsic criticism is the way of reading that puts texts firmly into their historical context. This is why the extrinsic attitude is often referred to as *historicist*. Historicist criticism, and there are many versions of it, uses literary texts to explore or discuss historical issues, and conversely it uses history and context to explain literary texts. In dealing with

Shakespeare's *King Lear*, for example, a historicist critic might look through the play to find clues about what was expected of a king at the time Shakespeare was writing, and how the ruler and the nation were thought to be woven together. By the same token, a historicist critic might also use evidence from Shakespeare's time and its historical context to explain the play. But historicist criticism is not limited to works from the past: you could use another form of historical criticism to study a contemporary popular novel – a 'bestseller'. Looking at the way people behave in the novel, even if it might not be considered a great work of art, would reveal all sorts of interesting contemporary social attitudes. If the leading female character, for example, is constantly and obsessively counting the calories she consumes, units of alcohol she drinks and number of cigarettes she smokes, this might indicate, for example, how strongly women in contemporary Western society feel forced to live up to an 'ideal' model of body-shape and behaviour.

Many of the newer ways of reading are based on the extrinsic attitude. Critics who use psychoanalysis as a way of reading might understand a literary text as a product of the author's psychology, or as a way of understanding parts of the human mind in general. In fact, the work of Sigmund Freud (1856–1939) and other psychoanalysts has been widely used to interpret literary works. Those who explicitly champion political positions use literary texts as evidence for wider historical and political arguments. The many forms of feminist criticism use literary texts to explore the roles of women and men, amongst other things. Other critics start with the text and draw conclusions about, say, nature, humanity or the pitfalls of love. Even approaches that consider the author's intention or her or his life display the extrinsic attitude, since neither the author nor her or his biography are actually *in* the text.

The idea of looking beyond a text to 'the world' is very attractive to those who emphasise the way in which literature is linked to the world. Many new forms of extrinsic criticism have emerged in the last twenty years or so as academics have sought ways of reflecting the changes in contemporary society. The emphasis on new literary theories at university means that you spend a lot of time learning about extrinsic approaches. The new assessment objectives for AS and A2, by mentioning contexts and different readers' interpretations, have also begun to move towards extrinsic approaches. Those who oppose extrinsic critical attitudes point to the fact that in using this approach you start with a literary text, but move away to an object or idea that is *not specifically literary*. They argue that in doing so you do not actually deal with literature itself at all, but rather with politics, the mind, history, gender relations, biography and so on. If you approach a text as if it were a piece of evidence for history, opponents say, then it is no different from a treaty, a will, or any other piece of historical documentation. If you read a novel to learn about the author, the novel itself is no more than a piece of evidence for a biography and no different from a diary entry. What makes the text special as 'literature' is not of interest.

Contrasting these two attitudes

Looking at the key aspects of these attitudes, as shown in Table 2.1 on the next page, is a useful way to compare and contrast them. These oppositions have been the subject of fierce debate and you will come across signs of this at different levels and in different ways right through the discipline of English. Both these general attitudes are valid, as are the critical methods they stimulate. Even if they do have 'blind spots', both have a role to play in English as a whole. Sometimes the most useful works of criticism are produced by a coming-together of these two attitudes in different ways.

Thinking about these general patterns helps to orient you by explaining why approaches to literature have developed in the way they have. This introductory guide to critical attitudes also makes it more straightforward for you to draw parallels between different approaches and to explore the presuppositions and blind spots of any particular approach.

Table 2.1   **Intrinsic and extrinsic critical attitudes**

Intrinsic attitude	*Extrinsic attitude*
Into the text	Out from the text to the context
A flat canvas	A window
Literature is worth studying in its own right: it uses language in a unique way	Literature is worth studying for what it tells us about other things
'Great texts' are the focus because they have artistic and possibly moral worth	Any sort of text is worthy of study, as they all reveal 'the world'
'Formalism'	'Historicism'
'Words on the page'	Context
Meanings often indeterminate	Context decides meaning
Practical criticism, 'close reading' and New Criticism	Historicism; psychoanalytical criticism; explicitly political criticism; feminisms; philosophical criticism; biography and other sorts of criticism
Text stands alone	Text only has meaning in context
Knowledge of the text alone	Knowledge of the context (history, author's life and so on)
Style, plot, character	Theme, setting

Summary

- One way to think about the presupposition of reading is to divide critical theories into two broad groups or attitudes: intrinsic and extrinsic.
- Intrinsic ways of reading concentrate on *words on the page*. A work is considered separate from the world and the focus is on its internal features. Critics who support the intrinsic attitude rely on language and structure to decide what a text means.

- Extrinsic ways of reading look beyond the text *to the context*. The literary text is seen as part of the world and critics move through the words on the page to broader, non-literary ideas, like history or biography, which are in turn used to explain what a text might mean.
- Both these attitudes have blind spots and gaps. Intrinsic approaches are criticised for assuming that there can be an objective way of reading and for separating literature from 'the real world'. Extrinsic attitudes are criticised for failing to see 'literature' as something special and preferring to discuss non-literary ideas.
- Thinking about these general patterns helps to orient you when you look at different critical approaches, helps you to draw parallels between different approaches and to explore the presuppositions of any particular approach.

3

The Author Is Dead?

- Who decides what a text means: the author or the reader?
- What is the traditional view of the author, meaning and the text?
- What are the problems with this view?
- How else can we determine the meaning of the text?
- Why has the author always seemed so important?
- What are the consequences of all of this?

Having looked at how we read, I'm going to move on to other debates in English that centre on questions of literature, meaning and how we see the world. Chapter 3 is about the relationship between texts and meaning, authors and readers.

How important is the author in deciding what a work of literature means?

At first this might look like a silly question: after all, the writer *wrote* the text and must have meant something by it. However, for literary critics this very question has been the focus of one of the most heated debates of the last sixty years. Roughly, the debate has two sides: those who believe that *authorial intention* – or what the author 'meant' – is central to working out the meaning of a text and those who believe that a text has no fixed meaning and that any understanding depends on the individual *reader's interpretation*. Perhaps the most influential figure on this second side of the debate was the

French writer and critic Roland Barthes (1915–1980), who wrote an article called 'The Death of the Author'. While the whole discussion is more formally known as the debate over the 'intentional fallacy' or over 'authorial intention', it is often referred to as the 'author is dead' debate, in an echo of Barthes's title.

For 'authorial intention': the authority of the author

> The Examiners are unanimously of the opinion that the proper interpretation of a first person pronoun in a piece of writing is to take that individual to be the writer unless there is internal evidence to the contrary. This is the only logical course to take. Teachers who urge upon their students the term 'persona' or invite them to use 'safe' phrases such as 'the speaker in the poem' cause their hapless candidates enormous trouble.
>
> (Associated Examining Board Report 1995: 27)

For these examiners, and for many people teaching and studying literature, it is 'common sense' that when a poem is written in the first person, 'I', then that 'I' is the author. They are claiming that any other approach is illogical, and causes confusion. It is even more 'common sense' that what the text means is what its author intended it to mean. However, 'common sense' is often the pretext for taking an idea for granted. If the aim of studying literature is to think about *how* we read, then it is exactly these sort of presuppositions that need to be examined. What, then, are the ideas wrapped up in this 'common sense' attitude?

Those who share this attitude believe that the text means what the author intended it to mean, and nothing else. The text itself, they imply, is like a code, in which the author has encrypted her or his meaning. In reading, the reader decodes the language of the text to find the ideas the writer has hidden within. A diagram to express this might look like Figure 3.1.

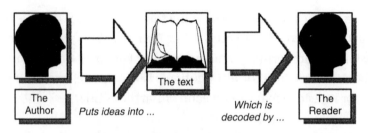

Figure 3.1 **The 'traditional' approach.**

This seemingly simple idea – that reading a poem or a novel, seeing a play, is just decoding what the author intended – makes at least four pre-suppositions that have profound consequences for the study of English.

(i) Meaning

If a text is understood as the encoding of the author's intention, it leads to the assumption that the text has one definite meaning, just as a code has a definite meaning. Once the reader has cracked the code, they have explained the text and have solved the riddle: they can give a final and accurate account of meaning and there is nothing more to say. However, works of literature often have ambiguous phrasing and seem to offer two or more meanings. Then people who argue this point of view suggest that the author intended to be ambiguous, and meant both things at once (with the implication that she or he was very clever to be able to do that). In general, this assumption leads to essay and exam questions like: 'How does Shakespeare convey the strengths and weaknesses of Othello's character?' If the reader sees Othello as both strong and weak, it is because Shakespeare intended it to be so. The assumption also leads to some interpretations of texts being described as wrong because they are not considered to be what the author intended.

(ii) Biographical evidence

If you accept that what the author intended is what the text means, it seems possible that you could understand a text without even reading it. Imagine finding some evidence – a letter from the author to a friend, for example – that says, 'I mean my novel to be about the conflict between good and evil.' Then you could say: 'This novel is about good and evil. I know this because the author said so!' It would be like seeing the original message before it was put into code. This sort of interpretation, autobiographical criticism, uses the writer's life story, through letters, diaries and so on, to explain the text.

(iii) Authorial presence

All these assumptions rely on the idea that the author is, in some strange way, present in the text, actually there. Through reading the text, you are in direct communication with the author. This assumption leads to questions like: 'In *Paradise Lost* Book 1, does Milton convince you that Satan is both attractive and corrupt?' This ghostly presence of the author is the final 'authority' that can decide what the text means.

(iv) Simple evaluation

Once it is known what the author intended and so what the text means, it is possible to judge the text by how well the author achieved what she or he set out to do. This assumes that judging a work of literature is like judging someone in a race. If you know the sprinter intends to run 100 metres in 10 seconds, you can judge whether she or he fails to live up to her or his intention. If you know what an author intended to do, you can ask questions like: 'How successfully does Jane Austen show the growth of her female characters?'

While many forms of interpretation rely upon this idea of authorial intention, and it might appear to be 'common sense', it has been criticised for a range of reasons. These criticisms are outlined below.

Against 'authorial intention': the death of the author

I have argued throughout that texts are always *interpreted* and open to different interpretations, stemming from readers' different world-views. The idea that by uncovering the authorial intention it is possible to find out the 'true meaning' or the 'right answer' runs directly against this and underlies all the major objections to authorial intention.

(i) Meaning: is literature a code?

Is literature simply a code? Certainly, this is the impression given to many students of 'traditional' English courses, such as the 'old' A-level. It is taken for granted that literature is about something – the 'theme' – and that the job of the student is to discover what this theme might be. So is this really the case?

I would argue absolutely not, for (at least) two reasons. First, the idea is self-contradictory. If literary texts were simply codes, then, paradoxically, literature wouldn't need to exist. Wouldn't it be much simpler to convey a message in a straightforward way, rather than turn it into a work of fiction? Why write a novel to say 'war is evil' when you could just say it, or go on a demonstration, or form a political party, or lobby (or even become) your own representative in government? Of course, there are texts with polemical messages, but when you respond to the message – for example, 'imperialism is wrong' – it's the message or the argument you are responding to, not the work of literature itself.

But there is a more important reason why literature is not simply a code to be worked out. A code works like this: two (or more) people share a cipher where, for example, the letter 'A' is represented by the number '1' and so on. One encodes, using the cipher, and the other decodes, using the same cipher. Thinking back to Figure 1.2 (see p. 127), this cipher represents the 'same way of looking' at a text, so both parties are agreed that 7, 5, 18, 1, 12, 4, 9, 14, 5 is

GERALDINE

a name in code and not just collections of numbers. But, as I have argued, part of the point of literature is that it encourages different ways of looking at texts, creating different results. So, in fact, reading cannot mean *decoding* the secret message, because there is no shared cipher, no one set of presuppositions we all share. Could you really see a text in the same way as a nineteenth-century author? Or even how your classmates view it? In having 'many ways of looking' we have many different ciphers which lead to many different 'meanings'.

(ii) Biographical evidence

This is also very much open to question. First, reading a letter or diary is not the same thing as interpreting a poem or novel. It would be interesting to find out what a text meant to its author, but that is not the same thing as thinking about what it means to you. Two critics, W. K. Wimsatt and Monroe Beardsley, in a very famous article called 'The Intentional Fallacy' (1946) put it like this:

> In the spirit of a man who would settle a bet, the critic writes to [the poet] Eliot and asks what he meant [in his poem 'Prufrock'] . . . our point is that such an answer to such an inquiry would have nothing to do with the poem 'Prufrock'; it would not be a critical inquiry. Critical inquiries, unlike bets, are not settled in this way. Critical inquiries are not settled by consulting the Oracle.

Reading a text, interpreting a text, is not an activity that has a right or wrong answer. It is not like making a bet.

Second, whatever the 'oracle' author said is itself another text open to interpretation. A letter saying, 'I intended such and such' is not firm evidence. Not only could it be a lie, plain and simple, but it is also open to interpretation because it is written within a certain historical period, where certain ideas were dominant, and because we, perhaps centuries later, may know things that the author didn't (and, clearly, *vice versa*). Authors might have very astute things to say about their own work, but what they say is only as valid as what a reader might say in determining the meaning of a text. Interpreting their work, an author is doing the same job as anybody else looking at a text. Another way of thinking about this is to ask, 'Who owns words?' Wimsatt and Beardsley, discussing poetry, say that a text 'is detached from the author at birth and goes about the world beyond his power to intend about it or control it'. They argue that authors might shape language, but that ultimately it is public property and readers may make of it what they will. This is not a modern idea: at the end of his long poem, *Troilus and Cressidye,* Geoffrey Chaucer (c. 1343/4–1400) wrote 'go little book, go'. He knew that, once created, the poem was out of his hands, and people were free to interpret it in any way they wished.

If an author's comments about intention are not authoritative, biographies are even less useful, being, after all, only an interpretation of somebody's life. It will certainly inform the reader about the author and her or his period, but will not provide a 'correct interpretation' for a literary text.

(iii) Authorial presence

Authorial presence is perhaps the most difficult assumption to understand. The question 'In *Paradise Lost* Book 1, does Milton convince you that Satan is both attractive and corrupt?' and others like it are, in a way, very confused. For they conjure up the rather worrying image of Milton appearing to you and arguing passionately that *Paradise Lost* Book 1 shows Satan as both attractive and corrupt. Surely, it is the *text* of *Paradise Lost* Book 1 and how you read it that would convince you (or not), rather than Milton himself. A text does not magically bring the author into the room with you – writing is just marks on paper. More than that, the very presence of the writing shows up the *absence* of the author. If the author was actually there, she or he could simply talk to you: the written text itself implies their absence, like an empty chair at a celebratory meal. (Look in textbooks at all the moments where the text says 'As I have discussed . . . ' or 'We said earlier . . . '. In fact, none of these things are actually 'discussed' or 'said' at all; they are *written down*. Using the sorts of words that imply real speech is a way of suggesting that the author is actually there, present and talking to you. But this is metaphorical, not real. While you read this, I'm off somewhere else!)

Some critics argue that the author speaks *through* the text, but how could you tell when this was happening? In many novels or plays, several points of view are presented, for example through different characters. Which point of view is the author's? And even if there are passages written in the first person 'I', how do we know if this is the author? It is with such questions that Barthes's essay on the 'Death of the Author' begins. He finds part of a novel where it just isn't clear who is speaking. Is it the author's voice? The voice of a role the author is playing (as the narrator, or as 'the spirit of the age')? Is it always clear who, or what, is speaking? Is the author wearing a mask? Or, suddenly, does the 'real' author appear? His point is that if you are looking for the authentic authorial meaning through a moment where the author 'speaks', it is, in fact, very hard indeed to pin down for certain *where* on the page that moment is.

If writers are absent, how could we ever get to grips with the 'authorial intention'? We can't ask them and we can't even find out if there is a part of the text which was written to tell us 'what they really meant'. With the person irrecoverable, it seems foolish to try to work out his or her intention. Instead, perhaps, we should make what we can of the text.

(iv) Simple evaluation

Apart from the question of what you are to evaluate, if you cannot trace authorial intention, *how* should you evaluate? Who sets the standards? Does the question 'How successfully does Jane Austen show the growth of her female characters?' mean there is some fixed model of how successfully the growth of female characters *should* be shown? Or could you compare Jane Austen to another novelist of the period, Frances Burney (1752–1840), and judge who was better? The idea of judgement implies an objective neutrality that nobody could have and demands that everybody thinks in the same way. While it used to be thought that the job of the critic was to judge what 'great works' were and who the 'great writers' were, it is clear that judging a writer's 'success' is more a result of the way the discipline has developed than a useful task in itself.

With these new ideas in mind, we could redraw the 'traditional' diagram of the relationship between text and meaning as follows (see Figure 3.2). The author, in saying what she or he meant by her or his work, can be seen as another reader, with an interpretation only as valid as that of any other person looking at the text. The author is no longer the all-important figure: The Author, as the saying goes, is Dead.

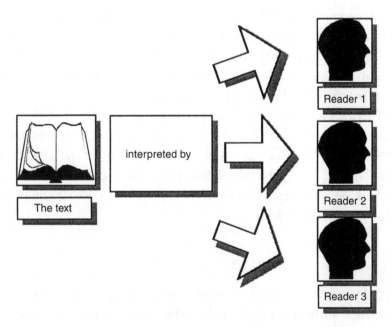

Figure 3.2 **After 'the death of the author' texts are open to interpretations.**

So why has the author always seemed so important?

Those who claim that the author is 'dead' also look at how the figure of the author was 'born', claiming this as another argument against authorial intention. The 'author' and the importance that the role has had in Western European culture was, like all ideas, invented. Of course, with broad concepts and categories of this sort it is impossible to say exactly when it was invented, but it has been argued very convincingly that this idea of the author came into being in or around the eighteenth century. This is obviously not to say that people didn't write before this time, but that their sense of identity as an author and their relation to their texts were different. Mass printing in England began after William Caxton (c.1415/24–c. 1491/2) introduced the first printing press in 1466 or 1467. Before this, who the author was simply wasn't important for thinking about what things meant. Medieval stories and romances were almost always without named authors (Chaucer is an exception). *Gawain and the Green Knight* is anonymous, but people read it without knowing or caring who the author was. (In contrast, if present-day writers stay anonymous it is precisely because it *does* matter who they are: they might want to escape persecution, or paying taxes, or scandal, for example.)

The concept of the author as the 'true source' of meaning perhaps developed most fully during the eighteenth century: the period of the Industrial Revolution. During this time of massive change, writing became *property*, something that could be sold. It was possible to have a career as an author without a patron, living by selling what one wrote. Since 'ownership' of the words was important to generate income, the importance of attribution grew. Another major influence that fostered the idea of the author was the Romantic movement – a loose collection of poets, thinkers, philosophers and writers in Europe in the late eighteenth and early nineteenth centuries. They focused on the created idea of the writer as *genius,* which didn't just mean 'very intelligent' as it does today. A 'genius' was a person whose immense creative and artistic power was a conduit between unseen powers (of Nature, for example, or the Imagination) and the world of human beings. Not only did this focus attention on the 'author', the genius, but it became important to know who had this special ability and who didn't.

The Romantic concept of the author also stressed that an author must be original. However, some people have cast doubt on the very possibility of originality. Whatever original idea an author might be trying to convey, she or he only has a limited number of pre-existing counters – words – to use to do this, just as an artist has only a certain range of colours to paint with. Even new colours are only mixtures of old ones and although the range of colours is wide – the visible spectrum – it is also limited (try imagining a totally different colour that *no one has ever seen before).* Like colours, none of the words the author might choose are new: words are the only system of meaning that the author can use. If authors want to explain what original idea they 'mean', they can only use words that have pre-existing meanings, so the words will already have *shaped* what the author can say. (This view reverses the normal assumption that an author shapes language: it suggests that, in fact, language shapes authors.) On top of this, much literature is bound by generic conventions, so any work has, to some extent, to fit an already established pattern. In a thriller, for example, the murderer can either be captured or escape. In a way, this doesn't leave much room for originality. These rules can be challenged and changed, of course, but this too relies on the rules, since rebellion has to rebel *against* something. These conventions are not part of the original intention of the author: the 'original' ideas are re-shaped by traditions of writing.

So the 'author' is yet another invented category, and even the way this category is defined, as a 'person who communicates original ideas', is open to question. But what are the effects of this?

Consequences of the death of the author

If the author is dead and reading to discover her or his secret hidden intention is no longer the only logical course to take, there are new questions to ask. Perhaps one of the most important would be to ask how one might understand the idea of 'author' now. The 'author' might no longer be the source of meaning in a text, but it doesn't mean that the term has become irrelevant. Knowing about an author does still tell us some things about a text: the French philosopher and historian Michel Foucault (1926–1984) coined the term 'author-function' to describe the way the idea of the author is used. For example, an author's name serves as a classification, as you can be fairly sure what sort of text, broadly understood in terms of style and period, you will find under the name 'Emily Brontë' or 'Stephen King'. This is not to pre-empt the idea of meaning but to suggest that the name is used to group certain texts together. The author-function is also used, correctly or incorrectly, to ascribe value to texts. When, every now and again, somebody claims to have discovered a new Shakespeare poem, there is more fuss than when a new poem by a less famous poet is discovered. Again, if you like the work of a certain novelist, you might buy another novel by the same writer. The author's name also becomes a 'reference tag' for other, often quite vague things like style or themes: critics discuss 'Aphra Behn's style' (1640–1689; British playwright, novelist and translator) or 'Samuel Beckett's philosophy' (1906–1989; Irish writer). Sometimes the names of authors are used as the tags for a whole series of 'big ideas' – 'Darwinism' or 'Marxism', for example. These ideas may have little (or even nothing) to do with those individuals in history, but the ideas still come under the classification of their name, so powerful is the author-function. In none of these cases is the author necessarily a source of authority on the meaning of the text.

Perhaps most importantly, the 'death of the author' – or at least of their authority – leads to what Roland Barthes called 'the birth of the reader'. I understand this to mean that a literary work does have a meaning, but it isn't a puzzle or a secret to be found out, placed there in code by a genius author. Instead, it's something that grows as an interaction between the readers and the text itself. Each reader is able – or should be able – to interpret and to produce an array of different and stimulating meanings. You shouldn't be restricted by wondering what the author really meant. The meaning of a text lies not in its origin, but in its destination: in you, the readers. Understanding a text isn't a matter of 'divining the secret' but of actively creating a meaning.

Nevertheless, the author's intention is still endlessly referred to sometimes to discount perfectly convincing and interesting readings of texts. It seems that many people want to find an authority to explain the text and provide the final answer. It is this wish for a final meaning that links the word 'author' with the word 'authority'. This desire is particularly heightened in reading literature precisely because, I would argue, literature stimulates an unlimited proliferation of meanings. This idea, taken seriously, can seem quite threatening. If thinking about literature makes us think about the world, and there are no right answers about literature, are there any firm answers anywhere?

Summary

- It is often assumed that the author determines the meaning of a text. However, the reader also has a role to play.
- The conventional way of understanding a text as 'what the author intended' makes a number of questionable assumptions about meaning, biographical certainty, authorial presence and evaluation.
- These ideas are open to question: we all read differently, and even authors can only offer an interpretation of their own texts. There is no one fixed meaning to be found or judged.

- The idea of the author is an invention, developed in the eighteenth century.
- The term 'author' does still function as an indication of style, genre or, perhaps wrongly, of quality. However, the meaning in the text relies more on your interaction with it than on the writer's intention.

4

Narrative and Closure

- Why are stories important?
- How do we understand narrative and narrators?
- What is closure?

Language is important in texts and in understanding the world, but we also use stories to order the world, and of course, story – or, more technically, narrative – is what literary texts are made of. A lot of 'theories' or newer approaches to literature draw heavily upon questions of language and meaning. However, there is also a great deal of work done on the way we use narrative to order and give meaning to our world(s). Doing English means engaging with and understanding narrative.

How are narratives made?

Part of the reason many people do English is that they are swept away by stories. They find books 'unputdownable' and read late into the night. This is part of the power of narrative. It isn't just books, of course. Soap operas, plays, films and in fact nearly every sort of text rely on this narrative drive, the desire to find out 'what happens next'. Narrative is everywhere. It isn't only in fiction: it is also central to each of our lives. When we are born (or at least when we can take notice of what's going on!) we find ourselves 'thrown' into the middle of things and other people's lives. In order to make sense of what's go-ing on, we tell ourselves stories. I'm sure that most of us have – when we were younger – done the same thing as the main character in the

Irish novelist James Joyce's (1882–1941) book *A Portrait of the Artist as a Young Man.* At school, he wrote down 'his name and where he was: Stephen Dedalus, Class of Elements, Clongowes Wood College, Sallins, County Kildare, Ireland, Europe, The World, The Universe'. This is a sort of story, about identifying who and where he was. And we are told, and tell ourselves stories about, what has happened to us or who we are and who we want to be, whether we write them down in diaries or transform them into poems or fiction or – more often – just think and talk them through. These stories are how we organise and sort out the chaotic world. They are how we give the world meaning. For example, if you are asked to tell someone about yourself – at a job interview, say – you quickly outline the broad story of who you are, where you come from and so on. You probably would not relate some anecdote from your childhood or describe in agonising detail your morning's journey. You present your story of yourself, organising the narrative and selecting what you take to be the most effective and meaningful facts. This 'organising' is a way of *constructing* the story of yourself: an activity that everybody undertakes, consciously or not.

Because narrative is so important and so all-pervasive in our lives and in the texts we read, study, watch and create, critics have been trying to define and understand it for a long time. A Russian theorist, Vladimir Propp (1895–1970) studied folk tales and argued that each of these fairy stories was put together using some or all of thirty-one narrative motifs. In each one, for example, the 'hero would leave home' or the story would end in a wedding or reunion. In a way, this was just an attempt to make more formal what, in the case of fairy stories, is quite obvious: that Prince Charming from 'Snow White' serves the same function, or does the same job, as 'Prince Charming' from 'Cinderella'. His 'character' as such doesn't really matter (as long as he is charming, of course). What matters is his role in the story as the hero, the rescuer of the heroine from the villains, be they the evil witch or the ugly sisters. The villains, too, are only significant because of their function. Propp's ambition, and the aim of those who came after him, was not simply to analyse fairy stories, but to create a 'science' of narrative, or narratology. This would be a way of breaking down all narratives in all forms into their constituent parts. There have been many rigorous attempts to do this.

These attempts have had some useful results. Certainly, this 'scientific' approach to narrative generated some quite precise terms. For example, one term that is quite widely used is 'diegetic': this is a more formal way of specifying the 'world of the story'. For example, the London Borough of Walford exists in the diegetic of the soap *Eastenders* and Springfield exists in the diegetic world of *The Simpsons* but not in the real world. However, this project does seem flawed in a number of ways. In looking for general laws of narrative, narratology passes over the nature of specific texts and is interested only in functions. While this is fine for simpler forms of narrative (fairy tales, or rather formulaic fiction, say), it seems to miss out much that is valuable from other forms of text. It is also 'blind' to historical difference: as both Shakespeare and *The Simpsons* rely on narrative, narratology treats these two art forms from different periods, media and genres as if they were the same. Moreover, each attempt to analyse the text has a position with presuppositions: Propp chose to look at 'the actions of characters', while another narratologist, Gérard Genette (b. 1930), chose to look at the ways a novel uses time, exploring how the 'action' jumped backwards and forwards with 'flash backs' or what he called analepsis and 'flash forwards' or prolepsis). However, these approaches are neither natural nor scientific but arbitrary. One could analyse a novel in terms of *where* the narrative takes place and how the characters move, rather than *when*, for example.

However, this approach did focus interest on some specific issues. Perhaps the most important of these is the question of narration: that is, who is telling the story?

Narrators

While not all stories have narrators, most do, and most literary texts certainly do. Sometimes the narrators are inside the diegetic, that is, inside the world of the story. Often these are 'first-person narratives' in which 'I' tell the events that have happened to me, or 'voice overs' in a film. *Heart of Darkness* by Joseph Conrad (1857–1924) is a 'first-person narrative' as is the film developed from it, Francis Ford Coppola's *Apocalypse Now!* (1979). But if one person is telling you a story, this immediately raises questions of narrative reliability. How far can you trust the narrator of a 'first-person' story? After all, they don't know what the other characters are thinking or doing, and they are surely telling you what they think is important, and what they think is going on. It is easy to imagine a novel in which what the first person narrator tells us is going on and what is actually happening are different. Indeed, in both *Heart of Darkness* and *Apocalypse Now!* there are 'slips' between the narrator and the story they are telling, leading readers and viewers to suspect that the first person narrator isn't being entirely honest. For example, Marlow, the main narrator in *Heart of Darkness*, describes the vile activities of the Europeans in the Congo and yet seems unwilling to face – clearly – his own complicity with them. (Perhaps it is precisely this struggle between his need to 'confess' and his unwillingness to do so that gives the novel its particular and peculiar form.)

Sometimes, however, the narrator is outside the diegetic, and seems almost to disappear from the story that they are telling. This is 'third-person' narration in which he, she or they – that is the characters – do things that the (nameless) narrator describes. These sort of narrators are often described as 'omniscient', all-knowing, because they do seem to know everything. They can, quite literally, get into the head of the characters and tell you if they are afraid, happy, or if they are hiding something. Traditionally, most novels have this sort of narration: it is the narrator who begins *Pride and Prejudice* by Jane Austen (1775–1817) with 'It is a truth universally acknowledged that a single man in possession of a good fortune, must be in want of a wife' (but is the narrator being *ironic?* Even omniscient narrators are characters).

However, omniscient narrators do not narrate everything. Indeed, part of the power of narrative – 'first-' or 'third-person'- lies in the 'focalisation' of the narrative on or with certain characters. For example, a detective in a murder story may not be the narrator, but the narrative accompanies her or him, rather than, say, one of the bystanders, and only reveals what the detective finds out. The narrative often takes one person's side over another, for example, and who or what the narrator focuses on is very revealing. The story of a murder and its solution told from the point of view of the murderer would certainly be an interesting read, but would it be a detective story? The use of focalisation is very significant, too, in the way it can change what we think about a story. For example, in an adventure story, the narrative focuses on the hero, not on, say, the hapless guard shot dead by the hero in the third chapter. But if the focalisation showed that guard to be a character too, with his own hopes and fears, perhaps the story – and the murderous hero – would look very different. Perhaps the guard works for the villain because he needs the money for an operation for his ill mother, or because he comes from a poverty-stricken part of the world, and the hero simply guns him down. These choices of narrative focalisation shape the meaning of the text. Thinking about focalisation in this way is not 'new' but it does offer new ways to think about texts. For example, although *Heart of Darkness* is set in Africa and is in no small part about the colonial relationship between Africans and Europeans, and even though there are African characters, at no point is the narrative 'focalised' through an African character: the reader is never allowed 'inside their head'. Once this is clear, then other aspects of the novel and its context come more clearly into view.

Closure

However, these ways of analysing and understanding narrative don't seem to explain either its importance or why we find narratives so compelling. This is because they don't deal with the issue of closure. How irritated are you if you miss the end of a TV drama or the last few minutes of a football game or an episode of a soap? How irritated would you be if somebody cut out that last chapter of a book you were reading? Why would you be irritated? Because you wouldn't find out how it ended. This 'wanting to know how things end' is absolutely vital for all stories, from the longest Victorian novels to the shortest cartoons to the most recent Hollywood blockbuster. It is one of the most important things about literature and about life and it is called *closure.*

Here's a test to see how significant closure is: would you read a book or see a film if you knew that the end was missing? Probably not. This shows not only how important closure is but also how the ending of a story is already implicit in its beginning: because even right at the beginning a story has an end, a goal, a conclusion in mind. Stories are *teleological*: they begin with an end in mind. Despite the fact that it is so important, closure – this 'wanting to know how things end', this feeling of teleology – is quite hard to pin down and, like many things in English, it is often just 'taken for granted'. (For example, the basic conceptual metaphor – 'life is a journey' – is a teleological metaphor: by suggesting that a life is a journey it implies that there is a final destination which will provide closure for 'life's story'.) However, although we may not be able to offer a strict definition of our desire for a 'sense of the ending' (as a famous book by the British critic Frank Kermode named it), it is possible to see closure at work. Characters on TV often say that they need closure in their life ('I need closure in my relationship with Ross'). They mean that they need to finish one part of their life, tie up all the loose ends so that they can move on. And in everyday life, there are many events that are 'acts of closure'. Graduation Day at school or university is an event that marks the end, the closure of a part of your life. Funerals don't end the mourning, but they end the immediate period of grief after someone has died. We feel that these acts 'close a chapter'. This is a key idea in understanding closure: we *construct* closure just as we construct narratives of ourselves.

This is why closure is also one of the links between the stories we read or see and our own lives: they both rely on closure to make sense. This is how the American novelist Henry James (1843–1916) put it:

> Really, universally, relations stop nowhere and the exquisite
> problem of the artist is eternally to draw, by a geometry of his
> own, the circle in which they shall happily appear to do so . . .
> He is in the perpetual predicament that the continuity of things
> is the whole matter for him, of comedy and of tragedy; that this
> continuity is never broken, and that, to do anything at all, he
> has at once intensely to consult and intensely to ignore it.

What he means is that things ('relations') keep on going on (your school or college will still be there after you leave) and what artists do is decide how to 'draw' the events, what bits to choose and where to end. In this sense, we are all artists whenever we tell a story. Life goes on, with its continuous events and all stories, fictional or real, are made by decisions about where to end. Do you stop telling the story at the couples' wedding (a happy ending)? Or at the new husband's fatal car accident (a very sad ending)? Or the widow falling in love again (happy) but being broken hearted when her new love leaves for Africa (sad)? And so it goes on. For Henry James, the artist's choice is where and how to end, how to construct a sense of closure.

Nearly all texts use closure – it's how all stories work after all! Some end with a very satisfying 'tying up of loose ends': the murderer is caught, the wedding happens, or the main character dies. Others are less final and, in recent years, some texts have purposely tried to avoid 'closure' leaving lots of loose ends, unfinished plots and so on. An example of this is the short novel *The Crying of Lot 49* by the American novelist Thomas Pynchon (b. 1937). This novel in part concerns what might or might not be a massive conspiracy that the central character investigates: but she never actually discovers whether it is a conspiracy or whether she is imagining it all. The point seems to be that not only is closure sometimes a bit hackneyed, but to draw attention precisely to the way in which it is constructed, especially in fiction. But these sorts of novels only work because you expect closure, so they, too, are using closure, but in a different way.

Closure is a key term for studying literature and is vitally important for thinking about how the content, form and structure of a text shape its meaning. Knowing about closure allows you to compare different novels, poems and plays by looking at how they 'achieve closure', which means, really, how their stories work. You might ask yourself how a thriller 'achieves closure' compared with a historical novel, for example, or how conclusive the ending actually is.

The question remains of why our need for closure is so strong. Why do we want to know what happens? There is no, one answer to this, but much of the critical theory you will encounter in higher-level English studies will examine the issue. Frank Kermode suggests that, perhaps, because we know how the story of our own life is going to end – the way all lives end – in death, the endings of the stories we read or tell are like 'little deaths' that will allow us to come to terms with our own, real death. It might also be because closure is a way of constructing and imposing order on a chaotic world, a way of drawing our own circle.

Of course, 'doing English' is not immune to the desire for closure. The desire to come up with the right answer or the final interpretation is in part the desire for 'closure': the end of studying this book or that play. However, if closure is constructed, so are our readings and interpretations that rely on closure. Closure is unavoidable and necessary but, at the same time, has to be seen for what it is: a way of finishing a story or – in the case of doing English – finishing with a story. But literature, although perhaps based on closure, has a habit of not letting itself be 'closed up'. Because there are many different interpretations of texts, we know that a sense of closure, of a final answer, is a construct, and that an interpretation can be opened again, reconstructed or deconstructed by different readers in different contexts. So to think about closure is to think about our own reading and the ways in which we impose our own meaning on texts. When you're doing English, the texts might be literary, but we can also think about the ways in which we impose meaning on the 'texts' of our lives and those of others.

Summary

- Narratives are everywhere and are very powerful. We tell stories in order to make sense of the world and ourselves.
- Some critics have tried to develop a 'science' of narrative, which has helped refine discussions of how stories work.
- There are different sorts of narrators. Some narrators are 'inside' the story while others are 'outside', but both sorts of narration shape the meaning of the text.
- Closure is our 'sense of an ending' and is part of all narrative. Some critics suggest that we seek closure to impose order on our lives, or to come to terms with our own deaths.
- In thinking about closure we can also think about the ways in which we try to impose meaning and 'final interpretations' on texts.